ANTIQUEMAN'S
DIARY

ANTIQUEMAN'S DIARY

THE MEMOIRS OF
FRED BISHOP TUCK

Edited by Dean A. Fales, Jr.

Tilbury House, Publishers
Gardiner, Maine

Tilbury House, Publishers
2 Mechanic Street
Gardiner, Maine 04345
800-582-1899

First printing March 2000.

10 9 8 7 6 5 4 3 2 1

Library of Congress Cataloging-in-Publication Data

Tuck, Fred Bishop, 1867–1953
    Antiqueman's diary : the memoirs of Fred Bishop Tuck / edited by
    Dean A. Fales, Jr.
       p. cm
    ISBN 0-88448-227-8 (pbk. : alk. paper)
    1. Tuck, Fred Bishop, 1867–1953—Anecdotes. 2. Antique dealers—
    Maine—Anecdotes. I. Fales, Dean A., 1927- II. Title.
    NK1133.26.T83 A2 2001
    745.1'092—dc21
    [B]   00-052776

Cover Illustration: Known variously as "The Antiques Shop," "Tuck's
Antiques Shop," or "The Country Auction," this oil painting was painted
in 1909 by Kennebunkport's Abbott Graves (1859–1936), one of Fred
Tuck's contemporaries and friends. Graves often used local people as
models, and Louis Norton, another artist, is fifth from the left, while
Frank Miller, the local druggist, is at the extreme right. Courtesy of the
Louis T. Graves Memorial Library, Kennebunkport.

Designed on Crummett Mountain by Edith Allard, Somerville, Maine.
Layout by Nina DeGraff, Basil Hill Graphics, Somerville, Maine.
Editing and production by Jennifer Elliott and Barbara Diamond.
Scanning by Integrated Composition Systems, Spokane, Washington.
Text printing and binding by Maple Vail, Kirkwood, New York.
Cover printing by the John P. Pow Company, South Boston,
Massachusetts.

INTRODUCTION

FRED BISHOP TUCK was born in Kingston, New Hampshire, on September 22, 1867. In 1885 when he was eighteen, he became interested in buying antiques and for $15 purchased an old highboy in very good condition. When he brought it home, along with a spinning wheel, several brass warming pans, and a foot-stove, his father chided him, saying that he would be laughed at for his purchases. But within a few months Tuck sold the highboy for $75, and by the age of twenty, he considered himself "a full-fledged antique dealer."

Seeking a desirable location where there were people of means, Tuck went first to Exeter, New Hampshire, where he learned many helpful lessons about buying and selling antiques. In 1891 he moved to Andover, Massachusetts, where he set up a sale of antiques near the Andover Academy campus and was soon able to sell the greater part of his collection. In June 1893 he moved to Kennebunkport, Maine, where he set up a regular shop in Union Square, opening "the first antique shop in Maine" on July 1, 1893. The *Eastern Star,* a local newspaper, duly noted this event on August 4, 1893: "A new store has been opened in the building recently vacated by the post office. Quite a variety of antique furniture, dishes, spinning wheels, etc., are on sale. An upholstery department is connected."

In 1894 Tuck was advertising rare old china and featured "Blue Pilgrim China Plates" in addition to old armchairs and claw-foot sofas. He advertised his store as "a museum of rare and curious articles gathered from various quarters of the globe." An August 1897 issue of *The Wave* reported, "Mr. Tuck's antique store is a delightful place to spend an hour. A peculiar charm lurks in the atmosphere. The old-fashioned furniture, the ancient blue plates, the tall brass candlesticks and glass fluid lamps seem to carry one back to the days we read about when gas and electricity were unknown."

Tuck enlarged his shop during the summer of 1900, adding a workroom and fitting out two showrooms to illustrate an old-fashioned parlor and a New England kitchen. But at the beginning of October Tuck recorded in his diary: "Commence to drive piles and erect a building at Dock Square. Make plans for Colonial style, to build for a sales room, and also to have tearoom connected." On June 21, 1901 Tuck opened his second shop in Kennebunkport under the name "Colonial Inn," offering refreshments as well as Colonial-style antiques. The *Wave* reported that the building was "of odd design and unique in its shade of green. [It] is close to the drawbridge, and the rafts connected enable boats to land at any tide. It is almost the first building to attract the attention of visitors as they come in by train, but the interior is the great attraction. All the furnishings are for sale and are of colonial style—old-fashioned sideboards (one of very heavy mahogany, formerly the property of a wealthy family in Baltimore), magnificently framed mirrors, oddly carved tables, and antique chairs (including a set that belonged to the first governor of New Hampshire)."

The other local paper, the *Star*, had noted, "Mr. Tuck is rapidly getting his new building into shape for the summer. The furnishings are unique, and the building is an ornament to the village."

Tuck's original shop at Union Square had remained open, but in August 1901 Tuck held a "grand clearing-out sale," admitting that local interest in antiques was not as great as he had hoped. Tuck sold the Colonial Inn building in 1904, but the following year leased part of the building back from Lydia Perkins and Joseph Titcomb for his antique business. Another section was leased by the Arundel Social Club, a group of about forty compatible gentlemen that included Tuck and local artists Abbott F. Graves and Louis Norton, who gathered frequently to play a game of whist. The old Colonial Inn is now the site of the Lyric Theater.

In 1908 Tuck moved—literally—his original, now enlarged, Union Square shop next door to Hovey's Wharf, and it was at this location that Graves painted "The Antiques Shop," which shows Tuck conducting an auction with a number of local people attentively looking on. This painting now hangs in the Graves Memorial Library in Kennebunkport.

The York County Deeds Registry records thirty-one real estate transactions between 1903 and 1924 involving Fred Tuck's purchases of land and buildings in the Dock Square area, Kennebunkport Lower Village, North Street, and spreading out to the Seashore Company lots. He was clearly trading in real estate as well as antiques.

Tuck went south for the winters from about 1898 to 1914, first to scout out the possibility of expanding his trade, but also to pick up antiques. A trip to Virginia netted him seventeen mahogany sideboards in Emporia and the epithet of "Yankee" in Charleston, South Carolina. In 1906 he opened a shop in Camden, South Carolina, and in 1912 he had a winter shop in Aiken, South Carolina, where he had a minor brush with fame in the form of Mrs. William K. Vanderbilt, as you will read. Two years later he was temporarily in business in Pinehurst, North Carolina.

Over the years Tuck tried a number of different methods of promoting his antique business. In 1912 he became interested in issuing historical postcards, working with lithographers from St. Paul. He found that people who had nice, old furniture they would not sell were willing to let Tuck photograph the pieces and would tell him their histories. In this way he was able to produce the first set of historical postcards for the New England states. Some of the cards he had cut into jigsaw puzzles, which he offered for sale.

Somewhat similar were the scrapbooks Tuck made, each one a mélange of brightly colored printed pictures of antiques and historical subjects affixed to pasteboard. Some of the subjects featured were the New England fire bucket, the first post office, a field bedstead, a warming pan, and a sea captain's chest. The enterprising Tuck also sold spring water in patriotic red, white, and blue bottles, and he patented the first moth-proof garment bag.

Another addition to Tuck's business was the restoration, repair, and refinishing of furniture. So profitable was this business that he felt it necessary to hire finish cabinetmakers from city shops. "It proved very interesting to the summer visitors to visit my workshop," Tuck said. "It proved the rendezvous for many a visitor at our local hotels." Tuck's custom of having his cabinetmakers refinish antiques, removing original surfaces in the process, would cause heartbreak today on the *Antiques Roadshow*.

On October 8, 1927, at the age of sixty and after forty-two years in the antiques business, Fred B. Tuck got married. His bride was Alice Varney, an eighth-grade Kennebunk schoolteacher nine years his junior. She was the daughter of George F. Varney, a plow manufacturer on Route One South in Kennebunk, who lived off York Street. Tuck, a confirmed bachelor up until this point, had been renting a room from the family. From the mid 1920s on, Tuck had his shop in a Route One building once the shop used by his father-in-law. Tuck and his wife continued living in the Varney home, along with Alice's unmarried sister, Mary.

Alice Varney Tuck died on June 27, 1961, but Tuck had predeceased her, dying on November 3, 1953, at the age of eighty-six. He had been retired for some years, but his obituary in the Biddeford *Journal* noted that he was "an internationally known antique dealer and authority.... Mr. Tuck has spoken at local service clubs [he was a member of the Rotary] and has shown interesting exhibits of antique glassware, on which he was considered an authority." The local dentist, Dr. Milton Hall, remembered Tuck as "a gentleman" and "quite fat and happy."

Stopping at Fred Rouleau's secondhand shop on Water Street in Kennebunk, Maine, one day in the summer of 1982, my husband, Dean Fales, unearthed a transcript of a reminiscence written by Tuck, titled "Antiqueman's Diary." Dean's family lived in the Kennebunks, and he had known who Fred Tuck was. After discovering the

"Diary," Dean undertook researching and tracing the story of Tuck's life and gave several illustrated lectures about him, in the process becoming quite fond of Tuck, his account, and his view of the world.

While Tuck had called his work a "diary," in fact it is more like a memoir than a daily record. Tuck had hoped to continue it up to 1930, but instead it ends in mid air in 1915. Several copies of Tuck's transcript have been located, with minor variations. For publication purposes, one text was selected, and where there was further information available from letters and other sources, brief additions have been made. The Brick Store Museum holds a collection of Tuck materials that includes a diary and one of the transcripts.

"As far as we can tell," Dean wrote in 1984, "[Tuck] was indeed the first full-time antique dealer in Maine... and [his diary] is the only diary of an early antique dealer I have ever come across. In what seems a 'reluctant' field of writing, Old Fred did not mind blowing his own horn a bit."

Riding on the crest of the Colonial Revival, Tuck was a product of the movement and expressed his role in a very colorful, inventive, often eccentric, delightful way. All this and ice cream, too! No wonder Dean liked him so much.

Martha Gandy Fales
Kennebunk, Maine

ANTIQUEMAN'S DIARY

Young Tuck, celebrating the Fourth of July, 1885, in
Kingston, New Hampshire.

THE YEAR 1930 marked my fortieth anniversary in the antique business. My experiences herein noted are taken from records, diaries, and photographs which I kept for the first ten years. Such articles as have been written on this subject of antiques have for the most part been written by collectors, leaving the dealer out of the picture. My opening edition is to be a true statement of my experiences, covering my first ten years as a dealer.

I became interested in buying antique articles at eighteen years of age, and at twenty years of age I called myself a full-fledged antique dealer.

I bought my first highboy of Nathan Hoyt of Danville, New Hampshire, for $15.00, which I sold at a profit. This highboy, then 100 years old, stands out in my memory as the most perfect specimen I have ever owned, inasmuch as there were no cracks in the wood, no splits or joints open, all of its original makings intact; finally, carved sunburst drawer, tear drops, and leg points in perfect condition; even the locks, keys, and handles complete.

I still remember the joking and fun my father made of me when I brought this highboy home, together with a

Tuck's father (left), mother, and uncle, in Kingston,
New Hampshire.

spinning wheel, several brass warming pans, and a foot-stove. My father said, "You will be considered a good joke—that is, if you keep on buying these old things!" For in his opinion antique articles were a fad, and only the story of them in the future would be of account.

I took the joke quite seriously, however. I thought I would not buy any more antiques until I saw how I would come out financially on my first purchases. In a few months after this I sold the highboy for $75.00 to a prominent New York City banker, and through the influence of this man I was able to sell all the other antique articles that I had collected. This served in my mind to prove that antiques were saleable, and to people who were considered men of substance, both mentally and financially.

I have written in my diary under date of February 17th, 1890: Calling on one Mrs. Hartland at Epping, New Hampshire. She had several old-fashioned articles she would like to sell. I found her a confirmed invalid, lying in bed. She talked to me and directed the conversation to the articles in the room she wished to sell. The first was an open Franklin stove; the brass andirons and the brass trimmings on it were well shined. She said the price of this stove would be $12.00. She then showed me a cherrywood inlaid card table, and several old stool chairs. She said these might be sold some day, but not today. I saw that the whole matter hinged on whether I bought the stove or not, so I decided to buy the stove and then consider the other purchases. Later I sold this stove to a well-known businessman who, after considerable wrangling, paid me $28.00 for it.

On my way home from the old lady's I purchased a grandfather clock. This clock I found in an attic and upon examination of the works I found that wasps had built their nests into all parts of the wooden works, making it very difficult to judge its value. I saw that it was a Hoadley, made at Plymouth, Connecticut, that it had a line to be drawn down to wind the clock, and that it had a pine case painted red, probably made at the local undertaker's shop. However, I took a chance and purchased it for $8.00.

On my return home my uncle greeted me with interest, looking over my purchases and like my father thought I had been sold this time for sure.

April 16th

OLD SQUIRE BRADLEY calls to visit me at my father's shop. He is interested to talk with me, as he heard that

I was thinking of going into the antique business. Did I intend to make this a permanent or a temporary business? "In my opinion," he said, "the collecting and distributing of antique articles is an education in itself, inasmuch as the contact you have with people of whom you buy articles, as well as those to whom you sell, must be a very interesting study. I can think of no better way for you to round out your education in early manhood than to follow the occupation that you are now working into, as you will have to do principally with people of refined tastes, education, and wealth."

October 20th
RECEIVE AN INVITATION to a husking bee. As this was to take place at a very old homestead, I thought probably I might have some fun and also pick up or try to locate old things in the house or barn. Taking a horse and buggy, I drove over to the old homestead and on approaching the place I saw that the long barn was partially lighted by lanterns strung along the cow stalls, and that the people were seated along the main barn floor, already husking corn. It was a merry group of young men and women, together with many older people, all busy husking. Some were telling stories, others laugh-

ing, and the young people playing pranks by throwing the ears of corn at each other.

I at once joined the party and proceeded with the husking. I noted that some of the men were wearing a mitten with brads or spikes attached, while many of the people were using their bare hands to strip off the husks. Some were striving to fill their baskets first, as the hired men stood ready to carry the baskets of corn to the corn crib, and chalk down the amount each one had to his credit. Many of the young people, however, were eager to have the traditional red ear to their credit rather than a number of filled baskets.

After the husking bee had progressed for about two hours, all work ceased so that everyone might straighten up, rest, and walk around the barn floor. Some of the menfolks were invited into the back kitchen where sweet cider was being served on a tavern table. I spied several comb-back rocking chairs and thought to myself, "Here's some fine old furniture!"

After looking around a little more I returned to the barn for the last hour of husking. The barn floor was then cleared and made ready for the dance which was to follow. Just then an old, much bent-over man appeared with his fiddle, and seating himself on a three-legged stool, began to tune up. The boys and girls paired off ready for the dance, starting in with Portland Fancy, Virginia Reel, and polka. The dance proceeded for an hour or so, when the lady of the house announced that supper was ready.

Some twenty-five or thirty people then marched into the long old kitchen, where a very sumptuous meal of baked beans, brown bread, mince and pumpkin pies, sheet gingerbread, and hot coffee was in order. I was particularly interested in the furnishings of the old kitchen. I made note of the tin candle sconces on the walls, the huge fireplace, the irons before it, the build of the table, and also of the chairs. At a late hour the party broke up. I tarried a few minutes talking with Mrs. Blake. She said that she had many old things that she might sell. Would I call some day next week? This I concluded to do and made my departure, having thoroughly enjoyed the husking bee.

October 26th
RECEIVE A CALL from Doctor Dearborn who lives in Exeter, New Hampshire. He tells me that he is hunting for old flintlock guns; shows me an old flintlock pistol. Said he wanted long-barrel guns with bayonets on them,

and that the date of their manufacture must be stamped on the flintlock. I did not have any old guns or pistols in stock; in fact, this was the first time I had had my attention called to them.

I was very much interested to try and draw out the Doctor on the subject of antiques as he seemed to be quite a character. After having a half-hour's conversation with him I came to the conclusion that he had bought and sold antiques quite extensively. After looking at my stock of antiques, he became interested in a chest-on-chest of drawers. This I priced to him at $15.00. I remember his saying, "If you will deliver this piece to me, I will pay you $15.00 for it."

I said, "Where do you want it delivered?"

He said, "I live in Exeter, New Hampshire, and my home is known as General Washington's Headquarters, where I want the piece delivered. Can you take it over to me next Saturday afternoon?"

The Doctor then gathered up his flintlock pistol, an old powder horn, and a bag of Indian relics and departed.

The following Saturday I took the chest of drawers and started for the Doctor's home. Arriving in the square at Exeter, I sought out the old house, and going up the stone steps at the front door, knocked with a heavy brass

knocker on the door. After some few minutes the Doctor appeared. Opening the door a few inches he said,
"Oh! You have brought my chest of drawers!"

I said, "Yes, sir. Where will you have it placed?"

He said, "You will have to put it in the east room, I
think. And by the way, there is the groceryman, who
will help you take it in."

He then closed the door, presumably to keep out a
cold draft of wind that was blowing at that time. In a
few minutes I succeeded, with help, in placing the chest
in the east room. He then called to me to come in by the
fire. He said, "This is a very cold day. I should not be
spending $15.00 for old furniture. I should be keeping
it to buy birch wood for my fireplace. So many poor
people need heat more than they do old furniture."

He then unstrapped his pocketbook, taking out three
five-dollar bills, and handing them to me, saying, "I don't
know when I shall get my money back on this piece,
but probably not until some of the boarders from Rye
Beach come up to visit me next summer."

I said, "Do you have considerable trade with the summer people, Doctor?"

He said, "I have considerable company that is looking for antiques. Oh, yes, I expect I do make some sales!"

I again visited the Doctor during the latter part of the summer, and he told me that he sold my chest-on-chest to a party in St. Louis. He said, "I had to fix it up considerably, and I only got $60.00 for it, but that was the highest price I ever received for a chest-on-chest."

I said, "Doctor, what articles do your visitors call for particularly?"

He said, "I have calls for old brass door knockers; in fact, most all of my callers who rap with the knocker on the front door ask me if I will sell this knocker. I tell them I would not sell that one, but I may be able to have a copy of it made. So take a look at it and try to find some old knockers like this one."

I said, "Doctor, what can you pay for a knocker like this?"

He said, "I think I can give you $8.00 or $10.00 for one."

Bidding him goodbye I thought to myself, "I'll look around for old door knockers."

October 28th

ATTENDED AN AUCTION on the Newmarket Road. Purchased a fine claw-and-ball-foot Winthrop desk. Bidding was quite lively on this, owing to the interest of the heirs in the piece. It was bid up to $78.00, but as it was in fairly good repair I concluded to bid it off at this price. The next article I purchased was a pair of fiddle-back chairs with Spanish toe feet. They were of cherry and evidently homemade. These brought $7.50 each. A picture top mirror with the overhanging top and fitted with the thirteen balls, the gilding being quite bright, I purchased at $18.50.

November 18th

MY FIRST INTERVIEW with Lee L. Powers, a dealer in Boston. He sought me out as someone who would help him find a quantity of old dried apples! He stated that he wanted to buy several pounds, that they must be originally strung and that the strings should all be a yard or more long. I found upon inquiring that he was fitting up a New England kitchen in the Mechanic's Fair Building in Boston, and that he wished a large stock of old sundried apples to be used as a decoration.

This proved quite a problem to me, to find anyone that had many old dried apples, as dried apples are usually sold annually, with no leftovers in the attics. However, after four or five calls in the rural districts of New Hampshire, I chanced upon a woman by the name of

Goodrich who said she had a lot of old dried apples up in her attic; but the question was, how much would I pay for them? After some considering we decided to pay three and a half cents a pound, providing that we could see a sample of the apples and that there was to be a large quantity to select from. Miss Goodrich said that she would go up into the attic and bring down a sample and tell me about how many she had like that. This she did, coming down in a few moments with her gingham apron well filled with old dried apples.

We weighed this lot of apples and as I remember it, there were some twelve or fifteen pounds. I asked her how much she had like this. She paused a moment and said, "I want pay for this lot before I decide on another lot."

Mr. Powers paid her for the apples. She put the money in a teacup on the mantel and then went to the attic for a new supply. We decided to look around the house and see what there was for antique furniture, spying a very rare comb-back chair. This we decided to try and buy when she returned.

Presently she appeared, but she had no dried apples. She said that she couldn't bring them downstairs, and she wasn't certain whether she wanted to sell any of them—at that price at least. At this interval she went to the mantel and looked into the cup to see if the money was still there. Finding it intact, she brightened up a little, saying she would have to take a window out in the attic and throw the apples out of the attic window, but we must agree to pay four cents a pound for all she had, which we decided to do.

She turned to the attic stairway door, bolted it so we could not go up into the attic, presumably to see her attic treasures. We next took up position under the attic window and Miss Goodrich proceeded to throw out dried apples.

After the first fifteen or twenty minutes of throwing out yard after yard of old dried apples, Lee thought that we had apples enough. Were there any more to be had up there? She replied in a surly voice, "I am to sell you all of the dried apples I have, at four cents a pound. If you don't take them all, there will be no sale."

So of course we had to say, "Let them come!"

Miss Goodrich had to take out another window to get the racks out on which the dried apples were hung. Finally, in about an hour's time she stuck her head out of the window and said "I think that will be all, but I want my hired man to see them weighed!"

This procedure took another hour and we found that

we had two hundred and fifty-six pounds of dried apples, probably the accumulation of twenty years in her attic, this woman being such an eccentric character that she would never sell unless the market was just right, and evidently it was just right when my friend and I called to get a stock of old dried apples.

March 20th, 1891

I HAVE A CUSTOMER for my Staffordshire blue teapot. This, by the way, has the picture of Lafayette weeping at the tomb of Franklin on it. The lady who is interested is quizzing me as to the history, and any little facts that I may know about it. In referring back to the time of purchase and as to where I found it, I find that my record of purchase was from a woman at Hampton Falls, New Hampshire. She hesitated about selling it because of its interesting connections. She told me that the teapot came to her from the wife of the Methodist Minister, it being given to his family at their donation party. It seemed it was filled with tea.

"Possibly you do not know what a donation party is?"

"No, I don't. But it sounds interesting."

"I find that people, particularly of New Hampshire and Vermont, gave donation parties to their minister and his wife as they were settling at the parish. So this teapot was one of the presents that was given at that time, together with quantities of food. For instance, here comes a man with a salt fish, a woman with a bag of beans; others with sacks of flour, strings of dried apples; in fact so many articles that it is hard for me to enumerate just what they would be. I simply tell you this to show you how it was that the Lafayette teapot was presented at this time around these conditions."

My customer seemed well pleased. I have recorded in my diary that the sale was for $25.00 under March 20th.

April 6th

I ATTENDED an auction at East Kingston, New Hampshire. The first article offered was a small pine cupboard, standing on legs, about thirty inches tall. The front was ornamented with pieces of wood cut into the form of ovals, diamonds, and squares. These were fastened to it and used as a decoration. The wood was pine and oak. It seemed to me to be a very interesting piece of furniture and I bid it off for $2.60.

Taking this piece of furniture to the carpenter shop, I had a workman clean off the old red paint, for much old furniture was painted red in the days of a hundred and twenty to a hundred and fifty years ago. Having had it cleaned and some little repair work done on it, I placed it in my stock for sale.

July 25th

MR. FRENCH called this morning about a very odd looking piece of furniture, said he purchased it on the Mountain Road. Upon looking at it, I judged it was a homemade piece fashioned out of early pine wood. The design and shape were original with the carpenter who built it. Mr. French said that it was called a "bonnet boy" and that the top part was used to keep hats in, and the drawers below for hoop skirts and shawls. I concluded that this was a most unusual old piece, so I purchased it for $25.00.

August 20th

AL MILLER called this morning and had a set of six Windsor chairs. Said he found them over in Mrs. Woodman's attic. Also he had a slip of paper telling me of the history of the chairs. It said they were made by a carpenter in 1824, the carpenter taking his pattern out of an old print. The chairs were in good condition and were painted yellow, the base had cross stretchers curving in the front, thereby making a very strong support and bracing the four legs. This was an unusually fine set of chairs and I purchased them and placed them in my collection priced at $100.00 for the set.

On June 8th [1892]

I OPENED A SALE of antiques near the campus grounds of Andover Academy. The exhibition caused considerable interest among the student body, as I was there near graduation time. Many of the parents of the children who were in town naturally came to look over my stock of antiques. The first piece that anyone was particularly interested in was the old cupboard previously described. The purchaser, a clergyman from New York State, paid me $40.00 for it, and I remember his saying to me, "This looks to be a genuine antique, but possibly I have been fooled. However, I am taking it for what I consider a journeyman's piece."

Another article that I sold was an old-time sea chest which I had picked up in Newburyport. I remember the man of whom I purchased it as being very eccentric. I found him sitting on a milking stool near the barn door. In reply to my inquiry about old things he said, "There isn't anything in the house, but I think I have an old chest up in the hayloft that I might sell."

After a little dickering I purchased the chest for $2.00. The lady who bought this chest of me was much elated when she found a secret compartment of which I knew nothing, that contained a leather bootleg, with this inscription on it in white letters: "Seek to know others, but keep thyself unknown."

During the next few days I was able to sell the greater part of my collection, and with that I concluded the sale at Andover, Massachusetts.

From Andover I moved to Kennebunkport, Maine, in June 1893. At first I spent my time visiting the old homes in and about the town hunting antiques. Some of the people were very reticent about selling their things, while others were glad to turn their old furniture into money. I found very little maple or pine but did finally succeed in collecting some mahogany pieces, among them a fine old Hepplewhite sideboard, some rare old silver, and choice glass and china.

This sideboard was found in a coal bin in a cellar, having been packed away for a great many years. The lady who sold it to me said that she was not interested to have it around in the way and that one leg was broken off and the piece otherwise in very bad repair. I told her that the expense for fixing it up would be considerable, whereupon she offered to sell it to me for $15.00. She also said, "If you don't get out of it all right, you can have it for less." I at once proceeded to have a truckman take the sideboard over to my shop and after several weeks' work it was in fine repair.

In looking for a place for my shop I decided to locate on the so-called Clark's Wharf. There I opened the first antique shop in Maine, July First, 1893.

As soon as the summer boarders came I found my shop was proving to be one of the interesting places for them to visit. On July 10th I had my first customer, a gentleman who was very much interested in looking over my stock. He finally purchased the Hepplewhite sideboard for $150.00. The sale of this sideboard proved a good advertisement as it created quite an interest in antiques among the summer colony.

July 15th

A MAN CAME into the shop looking for an old cider pitcher. I showed him an old pitcher of Bennington ware that I had found at an old home in New Hampshire. It was called by the family the "old raising cider pitcher." He said, "I was born in New England but have spent the greater part of my life in Buffalo, New York, and I

don't know what is meant by a 'raising cider pitcher.'"
So I told him the following story:

It seems that from 1780 to 1840 in the various rural districts of Maine and New Hampshire the frame for the building that was to be erected on the homestead lot was first prepared by the carpenters in the neighborhood. Each sill and rafter was hewn and mortised by hand, and this part was framed up first. Then the sides or wall part were put together on the sill platform.

Then it was noised through the neighborhood that a raising was about to take place at six o'clock in the morning at Sam Woodman's homestead. The strong men of the neighborhood gathered on the spot to lift the siding, studdings, and shorings, first up one foot, then two feet, slowly gathering more help, until the side building frame was upright in place. At each interval after a foot or so was raised, blockings were secured, then the boss carpenter stood on an elevation and praised the advancement of the work and announced that refreshments were in order.

The pitcher was on a platform by a barrel of cider. Anyone in attendance filled the pitcher with hard cider from the barrel; all who wished drank from the pitcher.

My customer, after paying me $10.00 for the pitcher

Fred Tuck claimed that the shop he opened in
Kennebunkport's Union Square in 1893, in a
building recently vacated by the post office, was
Maine's first antique shop.

departed, delighted with his purchase and the story connected with its history.

July 20th

I WAS ENTERTAINING a group of ladies who had come from the Ocean Bluff Hotel. One of them bought a Winthrop fall-front desk at $60.00. She considered it a very good desk, but she thought she had paid a very high price for it. Other ladies were very much interested in old glassware. I remember selling them two flip-bowl mugs at $5.00 each. They thought the bowls would make nice flower vases, but had very little conception of what a rare bit of glassware they had purchased.

July 25th

HEARD OF OLD THINGS for sale at Wells. At Hall & Littlefield's stable I hired a horse and buggy and started for Mrs. Jones's place at Wells. The first old article shown me was a swell-front bureau, painted yellow, and used in the pantry. The drawers were filled with a miscellaneous collection and the top of the bureau was used as a mixing board for rolling out pastry. Upon examination I found the bureau was solid mahogany and had all of the original brasses. After some trading I purchased the piece for $8.00.

I estimated the cost of fixing a piece in those days to be about double the purchase price—in fact, that is just what worked out in this case: $16.00 for restoring, $8.00 purchase price, $2.00 for crating, selling price $40.00.

Going to two or three more places I purchased brass andirons at $5.00 a pair, shovel and tongs at a dollar each—in fact, fireplace irons seemed to be plenty throughout this neighborhood, many being broken and out of repair and cast away to the attic, as fireplace implements were then going out of fashion and stoves were coming in.

Just as I was turning around to go home I was attracted by someone calling me. Catching the words of "Mister, Mister!" I looked across the highway at an old tumbledown house and caught a glimpse of a young woman standing in the doorway of this old house. I turned my attention to this locality, and the girl's face lighted up very pleasantly as she said in a childish voice, "Are you buying old things?"

I said, "Yes, I am."

She said, "I have an old pitcher to sell."

I said, "May I see it?"

She proceeded at once to talk about the old pitcher. I could not see the pitcher—I could see only a pretty girl. After a few minutes conversation I said, "Where is your pitcher?"

She said, "Why, down there!"

Looking down at the foot of the doorstep my eyes rested on what she termed her old pitcher. I saw a receptacle that was evidently used as a paint-pot, as the so-called pitcher was literally covered inside and out with various colored paints. It also had a broom and a mop inverted standing in it. I should judge that the pitcher was twenty-six inches tall; it had a tin nose and a tin handle fastened to it. It is no wonder to me that I did not recognize it as an antique pitcher, and I thought at this time, "What is the girl thinking of, trying to sell what looks to be nothing but mere junk to me?"

However, I thought it a good joke and said, "What do you ask for your old pitcher?"

She remarked that she had no price on it; she was sure it was a real old one, and thought that she might get something for it.

I said, upon feeling in my vest pocket, "I'll give you two dollars for it"—for that was all the money I had left. I thought my interview with such a charming woman was worth the price I paid her. Taking my pitcher I bade her goodbye.

Carrying the pitcher to the shop at Kennebunkport, I put it with seemingly worthless junk into a storeroom and it was forgotten by me. Some few years later while making arrangements for enlarging the storehouse I came across the old pitcher. In looking it over and scraping off the paint, I discovered that the pitcher was either crockery or china ware, so I proceeded to submerge the pitcher in a solution of potash water, allowing it to soak, and thus remove the paint. Much to my surprise this is what I found: evidently an English-made pitcher of the early 1700s; three pictures, the Nina, the Pinta, and the Santa Maria, were etched into the china; there was an advertisement of shoeblacking and a picture of an Englishman in top-boots, resting his foot on a stand, and these words printed: "Bone Black Dressing, the best Blacking in England; used by the Enlightened Leaders of Taste and Fashion. Nothing but the best of Bones go into the Making of this Blacking."

It appears that someone had treasured this pitcher after it had been cracked, as there were straps of tin encircling the pitcher, holding it together like the hoops around a barrel. I had these hoops removed and the pitcher restored.

It was with a great deal of interest that I retraced my steps to the place where I had found it, only to find that the building had burned down and no one could tell me where the party that formerly lived there had gone. I never was able to get further history of the old pitcher. Some years later I sold the pitcher for $100.00 to an Englishman who was sojourning in these parts.

August 5th

MANY PIECES of old mahogany furniture are sent in to me for repairs — in fact, the repairing business is developing very rapidly about this time, necessitating my getting finished cabinetmakers out of the city shops. It proved very interesting to the summer visitors to visit my workshop — in fact, it proved the rendezvous for many a visitor at our local hotels, both men, women, and children often congregating there looking through the old pieces and inspecting my workshop. I became very much interested in noting the comments of the visitors as they looked, talked, and asked questions concerning many of the old pieces. I was pleased one afternoon to receive a call from an elderly lady and her two daughters. The elderly lady, carrying a lorgnette, inspected the articles carefully. She passed by two or three of my workmen. Calling to me she said, "What are those men doing?"

I said, "They are scraping and cleaning furniture."

"What kind of wood is that they are working on?"

"That is mahogany," I said.

"What kind of wood will it be after it is cleaned?"

I said, "It will be mahogany just the same, Madam!"

"So interesting," she said, "to interview workmen, don't you know? Are both of those men Italians?"

I said, "The tallest one is not Italian."

"What nationality is he?"

"He's Irish!"

At this juncture she seemed very well pleased to call in the children and tell them that she wished them to pay special attention to the wood, and the manner in which old furniture was fixed over.

August 10th

I RECEIVED a letter from a New York importing house. It seems there were antique furniture concerns in England who were exporting furniture to the United States to be sold at art stores and furniture shops that handled fine furniture. It was suggested to me that they wished to consign a number of pieces to me. Thinking well of the proposition I decided to allow them to ship me ten or twelve different pieces of furniture, I to try them out and see how English antiques would go with my stock.

In due course the articles came from the Customs House to me. I assigned a room to this collection and awaited developments, showing them in a few days with a great deal of interest—that is, on my part of course, trying to sell them. Several weeks went by and I was unable to make a sale; I was at a loss to account for not being able to sell anything.

A gentleman came into my place and told me that he was journeying through Maine looking for an antique shop and had at last located mine. I asked him what kind of furniture or what class of antiques he was especially interested in. He said he would like to find an old-fashioned desk. It so happened that I had a very nice old mahogany desk in the stock of English furniture, so I showed it to him, and from the first he did not seem to be a bit interested. He asked me several questions about it and then told me frankly that he was born in New England, and his home was in Denver, Colorado. He said, "I am looking for an old-time desk that was made in New England, something like what I saw in my boyhood days. I do not seem to be able to find it with you.

Allow me to tell you that when I want English-made antiques I will obtain them in England, not on my trip to Kennebunkport, Maine. I do not feel that you should select foreign antiques to be sold in America." He bade me a hasty goodbye.

I will say right here in this connection that I was unable to sell any piece out of my collection of imported furniture. Returning it at the close of my season to the consignor, I then and there decided that my collection of antiques would be of the early American-made furniture, and such has been my endeavor since my first experience as written.

August 15th

I RECEIVED NOTICE of an auction of antique furniture in several of the Massachusetts cities, so I decided to attend. There were various tables, stands, and chairs and a grandfather's clock offered. Bidding was quite brisk but the prices seemed low, especially when it came to various chairs that were sold. I purchased several of these, together with a clock and a bureau.

In a few days I received them, carefully packed. Upon opening them and examining them I found them to be fakes and reproductions, so it seemed that I got my first lesson through buying what I thought was real, and at bargain prices, at an auction.

August 17th

I MADE A SPECIAL effort to find sofas with claw feet. At this writing I remember of having on hand, repaired, and in good condition, four. These, together with tables, chairs, and stands and one bonnet-top highboy, made up my collection in the front room.

One day a lady came into the shop and said to me, "I am looking just for fun; I have no idea of purchasing. I used to live near here and now I live in St. Louis. As that is a long way off I would not think of shipping furniture from the East."

After looking around for a few minutes she remarked, "It must be interesting, collecting these old pieces. Now, for instance, can you tell me where that old sofa came from?" pointing to a claw-foot sofa made about 1810. This sofa had four claw feet with acanthus leaves carved up over the arm. It was a very good piece and really about the best I had of the four sofas.

I said, "This formerly belonged to some of the Thorntons of Saco, Maine. It came to me through a truckman who had it stored in Portland for many years."

The lady became very much interested in my story. I remember hearing her remark, "Is it possible? Yes—I am quite sure! I have at last found the old sofa that I used to play on when I was a girl. What is the price of this sofa?"

"One hundred and fifty dollars," I said.

She said, "Little did I think when I came into your shop that I should purchase anything, and now I am overjoyed to make out a check in payment for the sofa that belonged to my ancestors."

August 19th

CARNIVAL DAY at Kennebunkport. Entertain people who are visiting at the hotels. Sales for today, four pairs of brass candlesticks; one pair sixteen inches tall, $18.00 a pair, one pair twelve inches, $5.00 a pair, one pair seven inches, $3.00; snuffers and tray, $4.00 for the set.

August 20th

HAVE A bannister-back chair. It was an unusual chair for me to find. The lady who purchased the chair was very curious to know why the term "bannister-back." Sitting down in the chair she remarked, "I suppose it is because it is straight and upright! Can you tell me about the history of this chair?"

I told her that I had purchased the chair at Danville, New Hampshire. It came out of the first old church, that was built in 1785, and from the will of an old lady I had read the following: "I bequeath to my daughter Isobel the bannister-back chair that was used on the pulpit in this old church."

This bit of history connected wtih the chair so interested my customer that I sold her the chair for $20.00.

August 25th

I REMEMBER having several old brass warming pans which I had collected for two or three dollars each. Some of them were interestingly engraved; one in particular had a picture of a rooster, another a picture of a bear, another had fruit and flowers engraved on the cover, which was perforated. These four pans were displayed at the front door of my shop.

About the first person who came in took down one of them and remarked, "This reminds me of old Lord Timothy Dexter."

I passed up the remark and thought nothing about it, busying myself about the shop. In a few hours another man came in. Taking one of the warming pans to my desk he said, "Have you ever heard the story that is connected with the warming pans?"

I said, "I don't know that I have."

"Well," he said, "probably you have heard of Timothy Dexter?"

I told him that I had read about him in story books.

"Well, he was probably the only Lord that America ever had. He was rated as an eccentric character, who lived in Newburyport, Massachusetts. His occupation was sailing vessels to the West Indian ports, bringing home a cargo of rum and molasses. It seemed he was all right enough in having a load for the return trip, but he was in a quandary to know what to take down for a cargo that would be profitable. Someone told him in a joking way 'Why don't you make your cargo of brass warming pans?' Without much ado he started advertising and collecting warming pans, as they could be found in many a secondhand junk store at a few cents each, their worth being only for the old brass. The man who started him off on this project, after seeing him load his cargo, thought he had played a good joke on him — that is, sending warming pans to a hot country!

"But, as the story goes, it turned out a profitable venture, for Lord Timothy Dexter sold the warming pans to be used as molasses dippers, using the perforated covers as a strainer, thereby turning this cargo for a profit."

This story interested many people; through its circulation at the hotel, and as a result, I sold all the warming pans I could find for $5.00 each.

August 29th

RECEIVE MANY inquiries for Currier & Ives prints, camphor wood chests, and treadle flax wheels. Not having any of the articles on hand, I went over to Limerick to find some. I had no idea of what people would pay me for them, so I just had to guess at what I could offer for them. I find on my return I had eleven flax wheels, about fifty Currier & Ives prints, four tow combs, and a clock-reel. This collection of antiques decorated the platform of my shop for a day or two. It was interesting to note the remarks of the passersby; I wish I could have taken down their remarks, as I think it would prove interesting reading today.

August 30th

SELL A FLAX WHEEL. Purchase price, $5.00, to be shipped to California. Express on it, $15.00. Another went to Fort Worth, Texas. One was sent to Portland, Oregon. I noted the sale of flax wheels, and their shipments went to principally far points west.

September 2nd

RECEIVE A CALL for a picture-top mirror. Looking over my stock I found some with gilt frames, others in black and white finish. These picture-top mirrors were formerly sold throughout New England and according to the price that was marked on the back of those I had, at $2.50 to $4.00 each. The one I am showing my customer is priced at $15.00. She said, "I shall have to measure the space in my room at the hotel, as there is where I want to use it for the summer. Later I shall want you to pack it and send it to my home."

I reserved the mirror for my customer's approval.

A few hours after this a lady comes in to see about having her furniture crated and shipped, and, incidentally, to pay her bill. As she was making out her check, she remarked that there was only one thing more that she thought she might need, and that was a mirror. Glancing around, her eyes fell on the mirror that I had reserved for the previous customer. Asking me the price of this mirror, I told her that it was $15.00, but I had reserved it for a customer.

The lady said, "That mirror suits me first-rate. Have you received the pay for it yet?"

I said, "No, Madam, I have not."

"Then," she said, "the mirror is sold to me."

I remonstrated by saying that I should give my first customer the preference, whereupon she laid down fifteen dollars on my desk. Calling to her coachman at the door, she said, "James, I have bought a mirror. I wish you to take it down and carry it to the hotel."

She turned to me and said, "Mr. Tuck, a bird in the hand is worth two in the bush, and I wish to have my furniture shipped to California, Sunset Route, via New Orleans."

That afternoon the first mirror customer returned, having decided that the mirror was just what she wanted. Would I please send it around to the hotel? I told her that unfortunately the mirror was gone. A lady's coachman had carried it away in spite of all my protests that it was reserved. She was very much the lady in her reply to me. I tried to influence her to take some other mirror, but she bowed her way out and told me that I had probably lost a good customer. I never saw her again.

September 5th

HAVE A CUSTOMER for an extension dining table. The only table I had was mahogany and what is known as the "cluster pillar" style, having four pillars at the center, two of which separate when the table is extended to put in extra leaves. This table I remember purchasing at an old sea captain's home, it having been discarded and considered too much out of repair to be of use to him. The table evidently was the early Empire period, around 1820. I had priced it at $75.00. My customer, after looking it over and bringing his wife in to see it, offered me $60.00 for it. I felt that I should have my price for it, to which he remarked by saying, "I can buy a better table than that in New York City auction rooms, but I thought I should enjoy using a table that was purchased at the first antique shop in Maine."

Upon consideration I concluded to accept his offer. After selling the dining table, the next two or three days business was especially good. I record the sale of a Chippendale armchair with claw and ball feet, $85.00; mahogany dressing table, $90.00.

September 8th
A LADY CALLS for a field bed. I question her as to just what she means by a field bed.

"Oh," she said, "I mean a bedstead with a canopy top."

I told her I knew of several canopy top bedsteads and in a few days hoped to have one in my shop to show her.

Going over to New Hampshire the next day I made inquiries as to who might have a field bed. I was finally directed to Miss French's homestead, where I was very pleasantly greeted by her. She invited me into her parlor to see her field bed, the wood of which was evidently maple. There were four tall posts, two posts of which were carved. The headboard posts were plain, being made square and tapering from the headboard to the top. Over all was a gracefully curved wooden canopy framework, curving first downward, then up to a graceful bow in the center. The canopy, supported by cross strips of wood dovetailed into the side bows, became quite rigid, yet was still susceptible to being taken down and folded.

The covering was draped back to the headboard, and tied to the head posts, and the only woodwork showing was the carved foot posts that were very beautiful. I told Miss French I had a customer for one. Would she care to sell hers? And she remarked very pleasantly that she had slept in this bed for over forty years and she hoped she would sleep there forty years more. Thanking her for a very interesting interview I went away feeling satisfied that I had found out what a field bed was.

Upon returning to my shop the next week I had to

tell my customer that I was unable to find her a field bed. After a few days consideration I sold her a four-poster mahogany bed. This had quite heavily turned posts finished at the top with what is known as "Turk's-head" carving. This bed was sold for $100.00.

September 15th

SOLD A PAIR of turtle-back bellows, $4.00; shovel and tongs and andirons, a complete set, $20.00; sold a pair of Iron Hessians with decorations restored.

Carnival Day at Kennebunkport

MANY VISITORS drive into town. One load came from Biddeford Pool. I remember some ten or twelve people got off a buckboard. They seemed to enjoy my shop very much, and much to my delight I sold to one of the party a pink china teaset of twenty-six pieces, all being more or less perfect, for $50.00. Another party became interested in a cut-glass punch bowl, together with ten wine glasses to match; the lot sold for $60.00. Another bought a bead bag, $8.00. This bag was prettily worked with pictures of a church and a flower garden on the front.

A gentleman in the party became very much interested in a pair of old leather firebuckets with the date 1806, which I had found at Cape Porpoise. The gentleman seemed very well pleased to pay me $10.00 for the pair.

It was quite interesting to me to see them carrying away their purchases, unwrapped, so they could enjoy showing them without difficulty to their friends.

Trade continued brisk during the rest of the month. I found my stock depleted—in fact, I was about sold out, so the only thing I could do when customers came in was to make a memorandum of what they wanted, thinking that during the fall and winter months I might pick up something that would meet their needs, so I took their addresses.

October 10th

ANTIQUE BUSINESS very quiet for the past week. In fact my season is about over. All the hotels closed and few cottages occupied. This afternoon I received a call from Abbott Graves and J[ulian] Talbot, they having cottages on the river road thought they might be interested to buy antique furniture; that is, if I would make a low price on a clearing out sale. I at once entertained the proposition. Taking out my pencil I proceeded to figure on what the pieces cost me, hesitating a little, where upon Graves spoke up and said, "Oh, never mind the pencil; give me a lump sum in your head right off quick."

"All right," I said, "How about $600 for the lot?" I could see they were interested in buying my stock together, after which it would be divided between them. After conferring among themselves, they make me an offer of $400. We finally compromised on $450. Upon dividing the stock there was an argument as to who should own the sideboard, whereupon Graves said, "I will flip a coin, and if it falls heads, why I have it." This seemed agreeable to Talbot and after tossing the coin it came up tails, and Julian Talbot wins the sideboard.

The next day I cleared out the shop and delivered the stock, and the following day closed up the business for the season.

In a few weeks after this I looked over my want list and found that more than half of the inquiries were for mahogany sideboards. This seemed quite a proposition to me, for up to this time I had bought only one sideboard. So I started out to see what I could find. While I found several sideboards that I could purchase at fairly low prices, I doubted very much if they would satisfy my customers. After reading several items in the newspapers I came to the conclusion that it might pay me to turn my attention to the southern states to search for antiques and keep in mind sideboards, for I had learned that there were many sideboards for sale south of the Mason and Dixon Line.

My first call was at Richmond, Virginia, on a Mr. Biggs, whose shop was located back of the old Bijou Theatre. He was very pleased to show me his stock that was contained in one small room. His furniture was for the most part solid mahogany, and consisted of two or three mahogany sideboards, several tables, and chairs.

Asking him the prices of the sideboards, he remarked that he could sell them to a dealer for an average of $70.00 each, but that he knew of quite a number of old sideboards more or less out of repair, that could be purchased for $50.00 each. After having had a very pleasant interview with Mr. Biggs, of whom I purchased several pairs of old Sheffield silver candlesticks at $8.00 and $10.00 a pair, I made inquiries as to other places where I might buy. He replied by saying that there were no regular antique shops, but there was an auction room on East Broad Street where possibly I could pick up something.

Going over to these auction rooms I saw very little antique furniture. Most of the stock there shown was secondhand. The man in charge said he was liable to have some come in any day, as there was a consignment due to come in from Petersburg.

After some few minutes of conversation pertaining to the consignment I left and went over to Petersburg. Looking around the old city I walked into Bowling Brook Street and called on two elderly Southern ladies. They were reported to have what is known as a china-press sideboard to sell. This kind of a sideboard was new to me; I was very much interested to see it. Going to the dining room they showed me the sideboard. It was about eight feet long, and standing seven feet, six inches tall. It had diamond-pane glass doors which were finely inlaid with white holly. The lower section had wine bottle drawers on either end. The four square tapering posts had bands of inlay around the base of each. All of the drawers were fitted with the original brass pulls. Asking her what price she had on this piece she said, "I have decided to sell it for $125.00."

Thinking this to be a rare specimen I at once purchased it.

The next piece shown me was a mahogany octagon wine cooler. This piece was inlaid to match the sideboard and I purchased it for $40.00.

I then called at Mrs. Johnson's on Tabb Street, who seemed much pleased to welcome me into her old mansion. She said she had a four-poster mahogany bedstead she would sell. On examination I found the posts to be some five inches in diameter, which seemed a little too heavy for my Northern trade. I purchased a Sheffield silver tray at $10.00, several pairs of old silver spoons, together with a sword-cane with engraving on the blade. With these purchases I concluded my trip to Petersburg, Virginia.

Hearing of the old town of Emporia, some twenty-five miles further south, I decided to do some house-to-house canvassing in that town, going to some of the old plantations. Taking a bus at the depot I was driven over the river bridge and up to the village hotel. Registering at the desk, the clerk assigned me to a room remarking, "Is everything all right, boss?"

I, wanting to wash and arrange my toilet, looked into the empty water pitcher and said, "I would like some water in the pitcher," whereupon he grabbed up the pitcher and went out to the pump. Filling the pitcher and coming back, I heard him call out at the dining room, saying, "There's a gentleman from Boston up in Room No. 5. I expect he'll want supper."

After refreshing myself by washing, I went to the dining room and enjoyed my first meal of southern fried chicken and corn pone, candied sweet potatoes, guava jelly, and rice—a very satisfying meal. After supper I was entertained by the colored boys who called at the hotel and amused the guests by playing their banjos and clog dancing. I, feeling quite tired, adjourned to my room and soon fell asleep, and after what I thought was several hours I was suddenly awakened. There appeared to be roosters crowing. Looking out of the window, I thought it must be near daylight, but I discovered it was only midnight, but the full moon was rising. I returned to bed and to sleep only to be awakened by heavy knocking on my door and a voice saying, "It's seven o'clock, boss, and breakfast is on the table, sir." Making my toilet, I went down to the office and inquired of the proprietor how it was that roosters crowed in the middle of the night.

He replied, "Oh, they crow 'most all night when it is moonlight in the southland."

Shortly after breakfast I started out afoot searching for antiques, deciding to do some house-to-house canvassing and visiting some of the old plantation homes. At the first place I called, the gentleman in charge said there were several "old-timey" pieces of furniture down at the quarters buildings. Here I saw two old mahogany sideboards, one Empire of the 1830 period—it had two pillar posts ending with claw feet—this I purchased for $10.00. The other was Sheraton with four fluted pillar posts on the front, four doors and three drawers at the top, veneered mahogany. The piece was in very bad condition. I paid $25.00 for it. This was all I concluded to purchase at the quarters building.

Returning to the homestead—this by the way was a fine old colonial mansion, having a broad piazza and several steps leading up to the front door. Entering the hall I was shown a claw-and-ball-foot library table; this I was very much pleased with, and inquired of the gentleman if he would care to sell it. He remarked, "I do not want to sell any furniture that is in my home."

He then went to the porch and pointing said, "Outside in yonder henhouse there is an old tray; I would be glad to sell that."

Upon looking around I found the tray partly buried in corn and grain. I offered him $8.00 for it; this he seemed pleased to accept. I was also well satisfied as I had purchased a genuine old Sheffield plated tray measuring 24 inches by 14 wide. It had the heavy grapevine design border that was still showing the silver. Having completed my purchases at this gentleman's home, he was very kind to direct me to a Mr. Melvin's home located "down the road." Calling there I found three very old sideboards stored under the back porch. They were Empire and in a very bad condition. The lady in charge said she would dispose of these "old-timey" things for $10.00 each. Purchasing these, I continued my canvassing still farther down the road; and after calling at four or five more old homes I found that I had purchased fourteen mahogany sideboards. Deciding I had enough, I returned to the hotel, and note in my Diary that the sideboards purchased in Emporia, Virginia, cost me on an average of $25.00 each.

I proceeded to have the sideboards crated and shipped to Boston, Massachusetts, via Merchant's and Miner's Transportation Company, from Norfolk, Virginia.

November 8th, 1898
RECORD THE SELLING of three sideboards to a dealer in Boston at $250.00 for the lot. Shipped the balance to Kennebunkport. Cabinetmakers were then available at $4.00 a day for eight hours' work. Proceeded to have them restore my sideboards. Many of the sideboards

came out very nicely, showing the white holly inlay that was not formerly observed. I remember having nine ready for my customers on opening my summer shop in June 1899.

This week I received inquiry for old blue historical china. I have several letters from people who have started collecting this ware. My stock consisted of ten eight-inch blue plates and four dark blue platters. I remember the views on the plates were of Harvard College, the old Boston State House with the calash in front, and those showing the cows on the Common, Nahant Hotel, and the Cadmus. The platters showed a view of Fairmount Park near Philadelphia, also a view on the Hudson River. This seemed to me quite an interesting collection. I found that the potters were Enoch Wood & Sons, Stubbs & Kent, and T. Riley, whose marks were imprinted under the glaze.

July 1st
FIND MY FIRST blue plate, "Landing of the Pilgrims," ten-inch diameter, perfect specimen; also have a three-piece set of dark blue china, pictures of Mount Vernon, made at Longport, English imprint.

July 20th

SELL MY COLLECTION of blue plates to a dealer from
New Jersey; average price, $10.00 each. My customer
was very much pleased and wished me to report to him
of any new finds.

The next day had a customer for sideboards. The man
was looking for two Sheraton sideboards; I showed him
several that came from my Emporia collection. Record
a sale of two for $285.00. They were sent to Rochester,
New York.

As the season progresses I find that the interest is for
the most part in small articles, such as light stands, candle tables, and small chests of drawers, customers telling me that as they live in apartments they cannot use
the large Southern style of furniture of which I had collected so many pieces.

July 25th, 1899

RECORD THE SALE of a small serpentine-front bureau
with old brasses, price $100.00; pair of mahogany can-
dlestands with oval tops, inlaid centerpiece, tops tip
up, price $50.00 for the pair; sell a set of folding tables,
the largest one thirty-two inches tall, next one twenty-
eight inches, next twenty-six, and the last twenty-four,

the lot sliding together, taking one table's space; sell the next for $34.00.

August 5th

SALE OF MOTHER HUBBARD wing chair, sold as is, in the rough, $60.00; also a Martha Washington mahogany armchair, $65.00. Interest seems to be centered on pictures and prints. I find in my collection many N. Currier, Currier & Ives, some of Kellogg's, and J. H. Buffum. These were the common old prints that were found among the households throughout New England at this time. My customers would not pay very much for them. I record my sales as about $2.50 each for those that were clean and well mounted. I see that $5.00 is the highest price that I received for any of these prints.

August 10th

HAVE A CALL for old braided or hooked rugs, then commonly called drawn-in rugs. As I did not have any of the rugs in stock, I made inquiries among some of the people who owned them, purchasing a number for two and three dollars each. Showing these to the customers, they decided that they were not the kind of rugs they wanted. Could I get some new ones? After some advertising I had quite a number of hooked and braided rugs brought in to me that I might sell on consignment. The next few days I tried to sell the lot but I was not successful in getting a customer—in fact, I did not sell any of the rugs that were left with me. It seemed that the price of $5.00 was not attractive.

August 12th
RECORD THE SALE of a six-legged highboy. This is the first one of the type I had owned; it had a six-legged base, urn-shaped turnings, cross-stretchers, bun feet. The top part had five drawers, three long and two short. It was of walnut wood, having burl walnut veneer on the front of the drawers, fitted with tear-drop brass handles or pulls as they were then called. The piece I considered a very good specimen of early American-made furniture. I found it in a secondhand store in Portland, Maine, paying $75.00 for it. I didn't have to do any repairing or restoring as the piece was in very good general condition. I priced it at $150.00. There was considerable interest in the piece, but as I remember, most of the people who looked at it thought it was of foreign make, so they didn't care to purchase it. Toward the close of the season I sold the highboy to a Boston dealer for $125.00.

Receive a letter from a lady at Derry, New Hampshire, telling me that several pieces of mahogany furniture had come into her possesssion as wages for nursing services to an old man who had owned these pieces when he died. The next day I called at the old homestead and found she had a Hepplewhite inlaid mahogany secretary which she had tagged to sell for $25.00, a swell-front mahogany bureau, priced $10.00, a tall four-poster with fluted legs at $30.00, also a base to a six-legged highboy for $10.00.

She remarked that she knew nothing of the value of these old things, so had had her brother mark the price he thought they ought to bring. Would I care to purchase the furniture? Without more ado I decided to buy the entire lot and proceeded at once to have a carpenter crate them. By five PM I had my furniture in the freight house ready for shipment. I returned to my home thinking that possibly I might consider that I had made a good day's pay.

As my season was over at Kennebunkport, I decided to sell the remainder of my stock to a dealer. Calling on Lee Powers, then of Cambridge, Massachusetts, I told him about the pieces from Derry. He seemed very much interested and in a few days came to look them over.

After careful inspection and considerable Yankee trading, he decided that he might use the secretary and the four-poster bed. He said that his chief interest in the secretary lay in the fact that it was well inlaid, had original brass knobs, and was small in size. He could offer me $60.00 for it. He said, "By the way, I shall expect to sell it in the rough at $85.00 if I am fortunate."

He bargained for the bedstead at $50.00. This order he afterwards cancelled, as he found that he had several bedsteads on hand of a similar type. The remaining bureau and highboy base I had put in good repair and placed them in my stock for the next summer's trade.

October, 1899
START OUT canvassing second-hand stores for antiques. Find a nice mahogany dining table at Newburyport of the three-section type, price $40.00; a mahogany candlestand at $10.00. Look at a grandfather's clock on High Street, the works marked A. Wood, evidently some Newburyport clockmaker. This was priced to me at $100.00.

Go to Haverhill, Massachusetts. Purchase two chests of drawers in a secondhand store, $5.00 each. After getting the chests home I found in the drawer of one of them a fine old blue and white coverlet, nicely woven and in perfect condition. I thought this helped out the sale price on the chest, which proved to be painted softwood, and of not much account.

Go over to Georgetown, Massachusetts. Find a claw-and-ball-foot serpentine mahogany desk which I purchase for $100.00. Meet a man who has made a speciality of collecting old brass candlesticks. He said to me, "I want to show you my collection."

Going into the large open kitchen I saw many candlesticks, some in pairs and numerous single ones. Asking him how many he had, he said, "The last time I counted them I had two hundred and sixty, and, as you will see, there are no duplicates."

He had them all well shined and was very proud to show them to me. I asked him if he would sell them. He said, "I may sell them some time, but I think I shall keep on collecting, as the interest in finding different candlesticks grows on me."

I quizzed him a little as to his experiences in finding them. He said that he made it a practice of inquiring for brass candlesticks, keeping his mind on these, and paying no attention to other articles. He said that many of the people whom he called on were glad to sell, but one old lady made the remark when he asked to buy her candlesticks, " 'When I have to sell the things my ancestors left me, then I think it will be time for me to go to the poorhouse!' " Fearing I had hurt her feelings I left the old lady, and, crossing the street, I purchased this pair of candlesticks. "You will note that they are most unusual. They have the center pusher with a knob to work up and down on the outside of the stick, with a clover-leaf edge on the base, and they are about twelve inches tall. This is the oldest and prettiest pair I have."

October 10th, 1899

HEAR OF A Sheraton sofa over in East Haverhill. Locating the man who had advertised it for sale, I find him in his barn thrashing out beans. He said to me: "Yes, sir! I have an old sofa; at present it is stored in the henhouse."

Going to the henhouse I saw a Sheraton sofa with four fluted legs in front, and a straight veneered back-rail with a nicely tapering fluted arm at the end. The woodwork was in good repair, but the upholstery was for the most part gone. I asked the man what he would sell it for. He said, "My price is $35.00."

I thought this a little high, so after some dickering I managed to purchase it for $30.00, sending a truck for it the next day.

My antique business for the remainder of the fall and winter was devoted principally to repairing and getting ready for next summer's trade.

June 5th, 1900

I MADE ARRANGEMENTS for enlarging my antique shop, building on a workshop, and remodeling the buildings in general. After having my buildings put in good condition I had two showrooms fitted up so as to show an old-fashioned parlor in the front room, and in the back room a New England kitchen. Then devoted my attention to collecting such articles as were needed in fitting up the place.

June 20th

OPENING THE SHOP I found that the interest in antiques was not so keen as it had been, because the people told me they were buying reproductions, as the old pieces of furniture were getting too high-priced. One lady I remember, who hailed from Rochester, New York, told me that a store had been opened in her city with reproductions that were "perfectly lovely" and priced very reasonably. She might want to buy a few old things for her daughter who was about to be married, but she must wait and talk it over with her a little later. The people who came in for the next few days said they were "just looking" and I fail to record a sale during the entire week.

Week of July 4th, 1900

RECEIVE ANNOUNCEMENT of auction sale of antiques in Vermont. Decide to go up there for a few days to look around in a general way, to see if there are any dealers, and also find what old things the State might have.

July 5th

ATTEND AN AUCTION near Springfield, Vermont, at an old farm house located near a sugar maple orchard. The first things that look interesting to me are the old sap buckets, also two or three maple chests of drawers. The sale starts first by selling the buckets; not knowing their value or whether they might be interesting to people, I am reluctant to bid on them; but as the sale advances, many sell for six, eight, and ten cents each; I purchase a lot of thirty at ten cents each.

When the furniture is presented the bidding starts up lively. The first chest of drawers starts at $10.00 and runs up to $26.00. I note that two or three dealers are bidding. However, the three old maple pieces sell on an average for $20.00 each.

Then a fall-front desk in rather bad condition was offered, which I purchased for $43.00. There were several pieces of old blue china in poor condition; one lady commenced to bid at $5.00 for the lot; I left the bidding at $19.50, so I think she paid all it was worth.

The lady who bought the china came over to ask me if I would care to come out to her home to look at some of her old things. As the sale was to continue for a few days, I decided to drive with her to a very old-timey homestead some three miles back in the hills. Going to her house I saw at once that it might be possible to find good old pieces. She told me that she had lived there only two or three years, coming there from her Massachusetts home to live with her aged husband, who owned these old things that she was going to sell. Looking over the various old things, I find one grandfather's clock, S. Willard movement, mahogany case, apparently in good condition; this she priced at $100.00. Going into a storeroom, find a carved oak chest, the date of 1754 carved under the front keyhole, price $25.00; one maple cross-stretcher tavern table—this looked to me to be a home-made piece; I purchased it at $20.00; several pairs of brass andirons at $5.00 a pair; and one of the quaintest three-legged stools I had ever seen.

With these purchases I left and went back to the village, and while in and around the hotel that night I hear of old things for sale at Windsor, Vermont. Going over there the next morning, I find a dealer who had a few old things in his shop, and a man at work decorating chairs—Windsor chairs, as he called them. I said, "Can you tell me if this town of Windsor is where the Windsor chair is supposed to have originated?"

He answered that a great many chairs of this style were made in and around Windsor, Vermont, some over fifty years ago. "I do not know whether or not the term Windsor chair started from this town in Vermont. I have been told that Windsors came from Pennsylvania, but I think their shape is somewhat different from the Vermont Windsors."

July 6th

PURCHASE NINE Windsor chairs at $5.00 each, paying $15.00 for an armchair. Next day go over to Woodstock. Find many beautiful old homesteads. Locate some glassware, but do not succeed in buying furniture. Purchase a very nice old sampler. Find the people generally interested in antiques in this town; think they had rather buy than sell!

July 10th

VISIT BURLINGTON. No antique shops here. Find that a lady who works in the post office has been collecting. Interviewing her, she said that she enjoyed hunting up old things; would I care to look through her stock?

I spent several hours very pleasantly looking over her stock of old curly maple furniture. She had one set of curly maple chairs, also the finest swell-front bureau in curly maple that I ever saw, evidently a homemade piece. Purchase a pink china teaset, also two or three Currier & Ives prints, one being a view of Lake Champlain, large folio, published in 1862.

July 12th

GO TO FITCHBURG, MASSACHUSETTS. Look around here at the secondhand stores. Find a very nicely inlaid Hepplewhite sideboard, also a pair of inlaid knife-boxes, these being of the sloping cover top, price for the pair, $25.00. Go out with a dealer to look over the old things in the city. The furniture shown me is the Victorian type; didn't care to buy it.

July 20th

RETURN TO KENNEBUNKPORT. For the next few days business is quite brisk, selling five or six pieces that came from my Vermont purchases — in fact, I find that old things in their rough natural condition seem to have the preference just now.

Receive a call from a dealer who had just opened a shop at Saratoga Springs, New York. Had a very interesting chat with him. I remember we compared our stock and also the general condition of the antique business. I found that he was selling antiques of a different class from those I was handling. He told me that the furniture that he was selling was mostly of cherry wood, as cherry was used in New York State as one of the first woods to be made into furniture. Asking him about the prices that tables, chairs, and bureaus brought, he said: "Well, I think that $35.00 seems to be an average for me to strike on a general run of the various pieces."

July 25th

RECORD the sale of five pieces of furniture, $175.00, to be shipped to the dealer at Saratoga Springs, New York.

August 3rd

ALL OF THE HOTELS well filled with summer visitors. Antique business very good. There seems to be a scarcity of desks in the summer cottages; sell a desk for each day to the extent of five. This cleans out my stock of desks. Have a call for a mahogany secretary. Locate one at Goose Rocks; this proves to be a very nice old piece; sell it in the rough for $75.00.

Find a nice maple gate-leg table. This, by the way, is the best one I have owned. Has very nice turnings, feet all on, and the leaves close with what is known as a "crumb joint." This table was very much admired and I remember the comments on it made by the people who came into the shop. One said, "Is that what you call a 'thousand-leg' table?" Another said, "That looks to be a genuine gate-leg table." Others remarked, "I suppose that is an eight-legged table?" I told them that I was sure it had eight legs! Then we had considerable discussion as to about how old it was. Anyhow, I told them it was a good old table, and I would sell it for $50.00. There were no customers for it this season, so I had to hold it over until some future time.

August 5th

ON RETURNING to my shop this afternoon I find quite an array of old furniture on the platform. As I was looking it over, Al Miller approached me with this remark: "Do you want to purchase this whole lot of antiques?"

I said, "I would like the gate-leg table and the set of Windsor chairs."

He said, "I cleared out a house at Goose Rocks and want to sell the lot as a whole for $65.00."

After some deliberation I bought the entire group of pieces. My curiosity was aroused as to his manner of transporting these twenty pieces, and found that he had brought them on the back of a piano-box buggy. He said he had the distinction of carrying the largest load of furniture ever transported on such a buggy. I had purchased the largest load of furniture for $65.00 that had come into my experience to date.

August 7th

RECEIVE A CALL from an old lady in the village. She seemed quite concerned about her old china teaset, because she had missed a piece each time she looked in the closet of late, and was wondering if anyone had brought in anything in the china line to sell to me. Not finding any of her pieces in my store, she said, "I would like for you to call this afternoon if possible, and we will go over my collection. Possibly I had better sell it—that is, I feel that way now!"

Calling on her after dinner, she took me to the china

closet, where I found a very beautiful copper lustre tea-set, in perfect condition, complete excepting three cups and saucers missing. She next showed me a cut-glass punch bowl, a decanter, and eight wine glasses, all beautifully etched. Saying, "I think that you had better take this lot of antiques over to your store, and I will come down in a few days and we will consider their selling price." I packed up the various articles and carried them to my shop, feeling that I had a much-prized lot of valuable antiques.

Having them on display a few days, the old lady came in and said, "I think I will set the price on my china set and pay you a commission for selling them. I shall want to net $125.00 for the teaset, and $75.00 for the glass set."

The teaset caused a great deal of comment, and a lady from Lowell, Massachusetts, purchased it, shipping it away as a wedding present to her niece. The punch bowl and wine set were sold for $75.00 to a lady from Cincinatti, Ohio.

August 25th

CARNIVAL and illumination night on the river. This has not proved a good day for selling antiques as the time is taken up by the people around the village and at the beach in decorating their canoes and floats. Also there is much attention by the cottagers and the guests in the hotels are trimming up the clubhouse where the decorated boats and floats are to start in a procession led by a band to proceed with the tide upriver to the drawbridge, there turning with the tide back to the clubhouse, where judges award prizes for the best decorated floats and canoes. The affair winds up with a special display of fireworks. It is four o'clock PM and people are seen coming into town from Goose Rocks, Biddeford Pool, Cape Porpoise, and many far distant points, riding in tally-ho coaches, buckboards, and hay racks. Special trains are run over the branch railroad and it is estimated that 10,000 people came to witness this noted annual event.

October 1st, 1900
COMMENCE TO DRIVE piles and erect a building at Dock Square. Make plans for Colonial style, to build for a salesroom, also to have tearoom connected. Tearooms are just becoming popular, so I thought it good business to open the first tearoom at Kennebunkport. This, in connection with my antique furniture business, proved very popular. Also, I find that the sale of antiques

In 1901 Tuck opened a second shop in a building he had built
on the Kennebunkport end of the drawbridge. He called it
the Colonial Inn, and in addition to selling antiques, featured
a "very beautiful soda fountain" offering "the best of soda
with pure fruit flavors."

Patrons of the Colonial Inn were encouraged to use it as
a gathering spot to meet friends for tea or lunch. Mr.
Tuck also provided a writing table and stationery free
for public use. The gentleman seated at the far left is
probably the proud Mr. Tuck, himself.

was very much increased by new business methods. Find people who have never paid much attention to old things come into my store, and generally become customers.

I was very much amused upon receiving my Colonial window tops that went into my new building, for when I opened the crates this morning, I found the window tops had been carved out of solid oak. It seems that there must have been some mistake, as it was unnecessary to use oak wood in their construction, so I wrote to my Swedish cabinetmaker—who, by the way, had only recently landed on these shores, and opened a cabinetmaking shop in Boston. I wrote him and asked why he had made my window tops of oak wood. He replied by saying that he had made them according to my orders. I failed to see how that could be so I proceeded to have him prove it.

In a few days he came down to my building and produced my letter. On looking it over I noted the words "O.K." on my acceptance of his drawing, and he in turn said to me, "Doesn't 'O.K.' spell 'oak'?" After that, I was very careful as to what I said in my letters, especially to Swedish cabinetmakers who had just landed in this country!

In checking up my stock that went into the new store, I find I have some ten or more old round mahogany tables; these I am to use for the tearoom. Also, I have tin and decorated iron waiters, to be used as serving trays—in fact, I tried to carry out the Colonial style. Each piece was for sale, and before many weeks had passed, I found that my entire stock of furnishings was already sold and listed to be shipped at various times in September and October, when the people would arrive at their homes.

The following winter I commenced to do a large mail-order business, dealing principally with people who have been recently converted to the lure of the antique.

March 8th, 1901

MAKE MY SECOND trip to the southland in search of old mahogany furniture, taking the Clyde Line Steamer bound to Charlestown, South Carolina. Find it very interesting looking through this old historic southern city; spend several days exploring same. Find one antique shop that had a good general stock, although the dealer told me that he could not keep many good pieces, as he was constantly shipping his best pieces to New York City. He had a fine set of Chippendale chairs; I remember the price was what prevented me from buying them. Also, he had sideboards, some ten or twelve dining

Tuck's Colonial Inn is on the right in this 1904 panorama,
and next to it is a new store he had built in 1904 and leased
to A. M. Welch, a dry goods dealer.

tables, and four-poster bedsteads with the very heavy turned posts. I do not remember ever having seen such large and heavy pieces of furniture before.

There were eight or nine mahogany wardrobes, some ten feet high, each fitted with two panelled doors. I remarked about the size of them and the dealer told me that they were taken out of the old plantation homes, from ten to twenty miles out of the city. People were discarding them, and just wanted to get rid of them. It seemed that there were no closets built into these old homes, and so portable wardrobes were used instead. Asking him if he had any sale for them, he said, "I occasionally sell one to people who are restoring an old plantation home. This also applies to those old portraits that you see hanging over there; the people use them for decoration, and probably allow their friends to think that they are their ancestors!"

Visiting another shop on Tradd Street, I found several interesting old glass punch bowls, also flip bowl tumblers and Toby jugs, the genuine old Staffordshire with the caricatured face. The people at their homes throughout the city seemed very loath to sell anything, and as a Northern dealer I met with considerable rebuff when I asked about them. One fine old Southern lady showed me with a great deal of pleasure a pair of silver candlesticks. She said, "Those, by the way, are the last things that I recovered from my old home when Sherman's Army marched through. I, as a little girl, grabbed these candlesticks, taking them to the back yard and burying them under the rose bushes. And now," she said, "I am showing them to a Yankee. Possibly you, Mister, would like to buy them?"

I did feel that I was interested in them, but I was more interested in their former history. I said, "What will you sell them for?" She could not at that moment set a price on them, but said, "It is possible I will sell them to you at some later day."

Going over to the old slave market, I tried very hard to purchase one of the standing stools used as a block, where the slaves were sold. This proved quite a problem and I came away unsuccessful.

Driving out the next day to Georgetown, South Carolina, I chanced on some very nice brass andirons, or dogs, as the southerners call them. I record buying some ten pairs, some of them being twenty-seven inches tall; one engraved brass fender, also steeple-top shovel and tongs, of the bell metal alloy, price, $25.00 the set.

Going into the country for a little ways and inquiring

at an old house, the man in charge said, "I think many of our old things are down at the Negroes' quarters. Possibly if you go over there you can pick up something."

So the next two or three days I spent exploring the Negroes' quarters. At almost every abode I was able to find something. I record one article as being quite numerous—a tilting swing mirror. This, varying in style and workmanship, was used to set on a bureau or on a dressing table; I remember buying fourteen in that neighborhood, all of different shapes and makes, many having no glass and much out of repair.

The next find I made was a set of candelabra, the crystal prisms being long and beautifully etched, the cast brass support showing figures of Romeo and Juliet; these I purchased at $10.00.

I went from here over to Savannah, Georgia. I find no antique shops here, but there is considerable interest in collecting antiques by the home people, the large and heavily built furniture prevailing, which does not suit my Northern trade.

February 25th

MAKE A TRIP to St. Augustine, Florida. This being my first visit to this said to be the oldest city in the United

States, I decide to settle down in the hotel for a few weeks' vacation, and the next day I run into a guide who is to show me the principal places of interest in and around the city.

February 26th

IN LOOKING OVER St. Augustine, Florida, I do not find any antique shops or stores that specialize in antiques. It seems that the exhibiting of antiques in the oldest houses is one of the attractions to tourists. After looking over the oldest city for a few days, I chanced in a secondhand store and looking around in the basement I found a bundle of old prints, and these, tied together with the cut that the pictures were printed with. Not fully understanding what the package contained that was tied up with old carpeting, I inquired of the dealer just what this old junk was, and he said, "Oh, I think that is a lot of old hand-colored prints."

After a little further investigation I inquired the price, and the dealer said "$10.00 for the lot."

Carrying my package over to the hotel and upon examination I found that I had over 200 old hand-colored prints, also the cuts of copper plates to be used in reproducing these old subjects. Showing my find to a New

York dealer, he said, "These cuts were probably reproduced from Ben Franklin's almanac, as they were the sayings of Poor Richard, so-called."

Finding them very interesting and having the cuts, I am using them as illustrations on several pages in my Diary.

Taking the train here I go to Camden, South Carolina, finding this a very quaint old Southern town of perhaps 6,000 population, with many interesting old homes, and the town full of historic interest. Going about, I meet some very charming and entertaining ladies, who were very gracious and took an interest in showing me their homes and telling me about the old-timey things that had come down to them. I found that many pieces of furniture were badly out of repair; these I could purchase quite reasonably, as they didn't care to spend money having them restored.

The first few days I purchased several sideboards, a dining table, and one grandfather's clock. I remember the dial had the moon changes, and on the face the inscription "Manufactured for Camden, S.C." This proved quite a feature when I came to sell the clock, as I found a purchaser who was particularly interested in any articles that came from South Carolina.

Over at the Weatherspoon House I purchased a mahogany dressing table, the four posts being of slender proportions and beautifully carved; this stood low to the floor and was fitted with a very nice old mirror. The lady told me that she was about to dispose of all of her old things, and she thought this a good time to let the table go.

On DeKalb Street I met Major Higgins, who was interested in showing me the old houses around the town. He was anxious to sell a tall four-poster mahogany bed, and would I go with him to see it? So we proceeded to his hotel, and in his room I found the bed of his description: a tall four-poster with acanthus leaves carved on the posts, and a beautifully carved headboard, which had been the property of a family in Gilford County. So, as there was no sentiment connected with the piece, he wondered if I would be interested in buying it for $100.00. I told him I intended opening a shop here in Camden, and would be very glad to start my stock with such a desirable piece.

Upon referring back to my diary, I find I did open a shop in Camden, November 1906.

Going from Camden over to Sumpter, South Carolina, I purchased a very fine set of Chippendale claw-and-

Above and right: Tuck enlarged his Union Square shop in the
summer of 1901, moving and adding an old blacksmith shop to
his store, and extending his display space to a wooden porch
that ran along the buildings and adding two new showrooms,
furnished as period rooms. In 1908 he would move these
buildings to the end of the old 1785 Hovey Wharf.

COURTESY OF THE KENNEBUNKPORT HISTORICAL SOCIETY

ball-foot chairs, together with a dining table. At another home find a Hepplewhite sideboard of serpentine front, six feet, six inches long, fitted with the wine bottle drawer. This piece seemed quite expensive to me, as I paid $250.00 for it. However, it was later disposed of as a museum piece at Washington, D.C.

Came across a Negro who was trying to make a business, picking up antique furniture. I found he had been quite successful in collecting, and I purchased several stands and tables.

April 15th, 1902
FINDS ME AT Baltimore, Maryland. Looking through the shops on North Howard Street, I find that the dealers report good business in old mahogany and Sheffield

plate. Meet a Doctor in the city who has a most wonderful collection of old glassware. I have a very interesting interview with him—in fact, I have seen here the finest lot of old furniture, glass, and silverware, that I have found on the whole Southern trip. The Doctor entertained me very nicely, and showed me where to find many articles that he did not care to purchase.

May 15th, 1902

HEAR OF AN AUCTION at Park Square, Boston, which I attend the next day. Find that many old pieces have been collected from Pennsylvania and sent here for sale. Meet a young cabinetmaker who is introduced to me as Mr. Israel Sack [who has opened a repair shop on Charles Street]. He is solicitous of taking in repair work, so decides to do over my corner cupboards, that I had purchased at the auction—that is, to scrape them and put them in good repair, for $28.00 each.

At the auction I purchased a set of six decorated Hitchcock chairs at $4.00 each. Hooked rugs were offered at this sale, but there were no bidders. Oriental rugs created quite an interest; I noticed one rug that was bid up to $875.00, and many rugs sold around $500.00 each.

June 20th, 1902

OPENING MY SHOP, I have many inquiries for pine
and maple furniture to be used in the summer homes,
also receive calls for hooked rugs. I became very much
interested in old hooked rugs, and the process of their
early making. I was also interested to find out why people preferred the old worn hooked rugs to the new ones.
In making a study of these drawn-in rugs I find them to
be the first artistic floor covering made by the New
England housewife. For the foundation, or warp, of
these rugs, gunny-sack or burlap was used. This was
attached to a frame, then, with a piece of charcoal, an
original design of flowers, ferns, or animals was
sketched. Old worn discarded blankets and clothing
were then treated to a vegetable dye made from the
roots, barks, and balsams in the forest. The dye-pot
was always in evidence in the home of the early settlers.
This dyed material was then cut into one-half-inch
strips to be drawn in or hooked in to the design on the
burlap, thereby making an attractive floor covering.
Many a rug was made during the long cold winter
evenings by the thrifty housewife. The originality of
design and softness of color is what makes the old rugs
more desirable than the new to collectors, and they are

willing to pay a greater price for the old rugs than for the new product. At this time I find that occasionally large rugs were hooked, measuring eight and ten and twelve feet. These, sometimes oval in shape, with designs of scrolls and flowers in the border, with a floral center, were among the rarest of old drawn-in rugs. No wonder these rugs, which took a year or more to make, are now selling for $1,000.00, $15,000.00, up to $25,000.00 or more. At this time of my writing I am unable to locate any of the larger sizes, although receiving several orders for them. Small-sized rugs, if they are well-hooked, are selling for six, eight, and ten dollars each, with twenty-five dollars as the top price for the better hooked rug.

July 25th, 1902

AS THE SEASON advances, I find a demand for maple furniture. It seems to have been a fad about ten years previous to stain all light-colored furniture mahogany. Now, this stain has to be removed to show the natural wood. Receive an order from a lady at Biddeford Pool to refinish her collection of old pine and maple furniture.

July 17th

ENGAGE THREE expert cabinetmakers (at $3.00 a day) to restore pine and maple furniture.

In 1902, Tuck noted that maple and pine furniture, with its mahogany stain removed and the pieces repaired and refinished, could be priced as high as mahogany pieces.

FALES COLLECTION

Antiqueman's Diary

July 20th

GO TO PARSONSFIELD, Maine, where I locate up among the hills an old deserted farmhouse. Seeking the owner I purchase the contents of the old house. There were five bedsteads, three of them with tall posts, with some of the posts fluted, several chests of drawers, tavern tables, and one pine corner cupboard. Taking home this collection to be restored by my cabinetmakers, I am surprised at the demand for this type of furniture; also, I am able to secure prices equal to the prices of mahogany furniture.

August 20th

ABOUT THIS TIME I receive a call from a gentleman who is very interesting to talk with, but I was at a loss to find out what he was interested in buying, or what he was particularly interested in looking at, as he was very reticent about making his wants known. Going around in the different rooms he finally came back to my office and seated himself.

"Well," he said, "I am not looking for old furniture or old china, but what I want to find out is will you go with me to visit some very old cemeteries in this neighborhood and in several other towns nearby? I am amusing and entertaining myself by taking down the old epitaphs found on ancient tombstones." And he proceeded to show me what he had found. I remarked that the securing of old epitaphs was indeed a new feature for me to start collecting. I was very much amused and after chatting with my caller I proceeded to get a horse and buggy and look up the old cemeteries of York County. I was very much interested in the search and in my companion's method of procedure. After a day or two of this particular antique hunting I settled back in my shop wondering what else would turn up for a peculiarity.

September 9th

MY FIRST VISIT to the Wayside Inn in South Sudbury, Massachusetts, calling on Edward Lemon, as he was the new proprietor, having bought the place from the Howe heirs. I found that Mr. Lemon was very much interested in antiques, and he told me that he was expecting to refurnish the property, as he contemplated opening a hotel and would serve chicken dinners. He was also fitting up a studio for his old prints and pictures. I record that he had a particularly interesting collection of small-sized oil portraits and sketches that he specialized in. This being my first visit to the old Wayside Inn, I made note of the furnishings that were contained in the house at that time. Mr. Lemon said that he should endeavor to refurnish the bedrooms and also wanted a complete refinishing of the old kitchen and fireplace. After visiting the old ballroom with the partition that could be opened up and noting the very attractive corner seats, I made my departure felling well satisfied with my interview with Mr. Lemon.

September 12th

HAVE A CALL for tin and pewter candlesticks and sconces. (This is the first interest that I have had shown me by collectors of tin and pewter objects.) Sold a pair of gooseneck forged iron andirons, also a fender made of forged iron that had a rack attached to it. This was to be used for cooking food before the fire.

About the close of this season I received a call for old oil portraits. I devoted my time to hunting for the same by going to auction rooms in the nearby cities. I had very little difficulty in purchasing quite a stock of them; some of the old portraits were what is known as "signed" pieces. These were bought by the better class of collectors at bargain prices.

September 14th

HAVE CORRESPONDENCE with a lady from Cleveland, Ohio. She wished me to send her three or four of what I considered my best old portraits, but they must be of either young women or old ladies. I sent her five, telling her to make me an offer on them, specifying the price she would pay for each one.

September 18th

THE LADY FROM CLEVELAND writes me that she will pay $25.00, $35.00, and $40.00 each for the old portraits she has selected, that she is buying them for the details of costuming and hairdressing, which would help her in her work as a decorator. Many of these portraits, being of the time of 1805 to 1820, would give her an authentic description of the styles at that time. At these prices I was satisfied that there was some money to be made in buying old portraits.

October

CHARLESTON, South Carolina. I notice a lot of old copper kettles that had been sent in to a junk store. Thinking that these might possibly be used for holding wood around the fireplace, I purchase several, and after having them cleaned I find that their color was very attractive when used upon a hooked rug in front of the fireplace. Record the sale of four different size kettles. These were shipped to Paul Smith's camp in the Adirondacks.

A few weeks after recording this sale, I receive numerous orders as it seemed that there was no one cleaning up and bringing out old copper kettles excepting myself. This morning after placing several kettles on display in front of the store, I was interested in noticing the attraction they caused, also the comments of the passersby. I remember the sheriff said, "You better watch out and put those kettles in early tonight."

"Why," I asked, "What's the reason for that?"

"Why don't you see, someone will be swiping them to make a still out of them."

Thinking no more about the matter at that time, but toward the late afternoon I was attracted by a typical southerner commonly known as Uncle Zeke. He was attentively looking over my kettles, and finally upon being questioned, he told me that he could make a good still by using about three of the different sizes. I said, "Will you tell me how you would go about using my kettles to assemble a whiskey still?"

Straightening up and clearing his mouth of tobacco

juice, he said, "Well, I should go about it like this"—
pointing to the largest kettle—"I should use this one for
the base, removing the iron bale, and then taking the
next size kettle, inverting the top, and having the two
soldered together; then cut a hole in the top part and
use a smaller kettle soldered to the top—this to be used
as the cap. After I have this much done I think that it
will be very easy to attach the worm, and this would
complete a copper still."

Thinking that this was a very interesting story, I was
pleased to note the old gentleman's way of making the still.

October 20th
THIS PAGE WILL be devoted to the first cut of Ben
Franklin's maxims, showing the interior of an Englishman's office, describing the furnishings. This will follow
with the maxim:

Creditors have better memories than debtors.

It is hard for an empty bag to stand upright.

June, 1903
SEASON OPENED at Kennebunkport with numerous
calls for bookcases. The Empire bookcase, many of them
six feet tall, have diamond pane glass doors and are finished with a scroll design at the top and fitted with two

This secretary, now owned by the Brick Store Museum, had a
chalkmark in a drawer noting "Abner Stone, Kennebunkport."
Although it may not have passed through the hands of Fred Tuck and
his craftsmen, it has clearly been modified from its original form. The
pediment was fashioned from the leaf of a drop-leaf table, and the
inlays were later additions. These were typical Tuck "improvements."

FALES COLLECTION

Antiqueman's Diary

This secretary has also been "improved." The pediment with its
unusual wave pattern is fanciful and unique.

FALES COLLECTION

This authentic secretary was built by Benjamin Illsley, who was in business in Portland around 1814. It is an example of what Tuck might have tried to emulate with his own creations.

FALES COLLECTION

drawers at the bottom. These were evidently made about
1830. I am selling them at $125.00 each, refinished.
There is considerable call for them and I find them
quite difficult to obtain.

July 6th
SELL A WINTHROP desk this morning. This desk was
of mahogany, and the fall-front lid opening shows a very
fine cabinet. This cabinet is fitted with Will drawers and
has secret fastenings. There is also a sliding well. These
minute details of a fine old piece my customer is particularly interested in; also the history of the desk I am as-
certaining from the former owners. My customer wanted
a chair to use at the desk. I told her I thought almost any
chair was used in the old days as a desk chair. I had
two or three chairs that were made by some of the early
cabinetmakers at Newburyport, Massachusetts, 1806 to
1810. It seems that chairs made especially for a desk
were very hard to find, and this is true even to this day.

August 12th
FIND THAT MY collection of some over sixty Chippendale mirrors is causing considerable attention. These
mirrors were made mostly in the old shops in Cam-
bridgeport and Salem, Massachusetts, with some of Eng-

lish manufacture, that had been imported. Frames average in size from fourteen to fifty-four inches tall, and ten to twenty inches wide. Occasionally I found one with an old bevelled plate and on examination I found that they had a peculiar bevel, unlike any of the modern grinding of today. On the back of some of the mirrors were the maker's label. This proved a special feature in interesting my customers. Prices of mirrors ranged from $10.00 for the small size to $50.00 for the large ones.

September 10th

I RECEIVED A letter from a New York architect who had finished a Colonial home for a New York banker. It seems that there was a certain place in the den that needed some Colonial china for a decoration. His decorator suggested that he use old Staffordshire pepper pots, as these would give a bit of color and attractiveness by their various shapes and sizes. His order called for two hundred and fifty pepper pots, all in good condition, with no two alike. He was willing to pay $5.00 each for the first one hundred, $10.00 each for the second one hundred, and $15.00 each for the last fifty, providing the order was filled in four months' time. So after closing my summer season, I started to collect pepper pots from the dealers throughout New England. I also employed a woman to canvas the homes, paying her three dollars each for all she could find. I finally succeeded in obtaining a collection of two hundred pepper pots, after many interesting experiences in collecting. My greatest difficulty lay in securing specimens, with no two alike. I was unable to get enough to complete the order, so my customer turned his attention to collecting in the English market. He succeeded in having his order filled promptly, but on close inspection of the peppers he discovered he was paying $15.00 each for a new fifty-cent article! And that to get a genuine antique he had to take the same slow course that I followed in making my collection for him.

Receive notification of an auction sale in New Hampshire. Having made some of my best purchases at country auctions I was interested in following up the sale, not knowing at what time or place I might chance upon different articles that might be of profit to me. Upon my arrival there I note two or three dealers who had come from long distances. They were in groups, talking intently over some plan that they wished to work out, so as to benefit the trust about to be formed. One of them came forward to me and said that he would like for me to come into his pool.

I said, "What are you proposing to work out?"

He said, "There is no use for all of us dealers to be bidding on one article, so I propose that we have one man to bid, and then when the sale is over we will draw lots, each one taking the piece that fell to him by lot, paying the price that it was bid in for."

I did not take kindly to the proposition, thinking that I might have some article left on my hands that I did not care to purchase, so I kept myself out of the pool.

The sale opened with a very interesting auctioneer, a typical Yankee with gift of gab, who stood on a stool where he could view the bidders. The first article offered was the old spinning wheel, which, after considerable haggling, was knocked down for twenty-five cents. The bidding continued with old iron candlesticks, five cents a pair, and many baskets, very old in pattern, sold at two cents each. Considerable time was taken up in disposing of a miscellaneous lot of rough antiques. The auctioneer then decided to offer some of the old pictures that were in the house. It seems that the former owner was very much of a horseman, and he had collected horse-racing pictures. There were over twenty of the Currier & Ives, large folio. Just before the sale on the pictures started, the auctioneer produced a paper which

read: "Race at the Fair Grounds on July Fourth, 1845."
Then he proceeded to sell the pictures. Bidding was
very lively from the first. A picture of Maud S., with a
record of 2:19, was started at $2.00, and sold for $18.50.
The picture that brought the highest price was of the
horse Flora Temple. I do not know what caused this
picture to go at a price of $34.00, but I know it was the
talk of the sale at that time.

The collection of pictures being sold, next thing in
order came the furniture that was in the front room. A
grandfather's clock caused lively bidding by several of
the city folk, and by one lady in particular, whose asso-
ciations with the family caused her to get quite excited.
Finally the clock was knocked down at $287.00. That
was considered a very high price and was one of the
features of the sale. The old silver chest was next brought
out, containing many spoons, knives, forks, and a pair
of interesting silver ladles. I recall that the spoons had a
shock of wheat engraved on the handles. It was decided
to sell the pieces of silverware separately. I noticed one
of the dealers who had formed the pool started the bidding. The sale progressed for a few minutes, the spoons
going up to five, six-fifty, and eight dollars each. At this
price my pool friend dropped out. It was recorded that

the sale for the silver chest netted some over $370.00.
At this time the auction was adjourned for lunch.
Crackers and cheese and mugs of hot coffee were served.
Many were standing around chatting and talking over
the prospects of the afternoon bidding.

The auction started up promptly at one o'clock, selling the furniture that had been in a bedroom. A four-
poster bedstead in mahogany was offered, and lively
bidding ran it up to $58.00. The bedding that was used
on this bed was next sold in order. First came a husk
mattress—this was knocked down for sixty cents, but
the feather bed that was made to be used over it brought
$7.45. Then came the old homespun linen sheets. There
was spirited bidding on these, as they were in good condition. They brought $11.00 a pair. The bedspread
caused a great deal of comment because it was made of
copper plate. The design stamped on the piece was of
an historical nature, showing some battlefield scene.
The man who was working the pool ran the piece up to
some over $30.00, but it was finally knocked down to a
Philadelphia lawyer at $37.50. It seems the lawyer had
purchased the entire outfit of the bedstead with all of
its furnishings.

The next thing in order were the bed-steps of mahogany wood that matched the bed and had been used by the owner in climbing into bed. The bidding became very active, as it was most unusual for such a desirable article to be offered at an auction sale. The steps were finally bid off for $19.50, causing a great deal of comment that bed-steps, even though rare, should bring such a price.

The sale concluded with the offering of a corner cupboard, mantelpieces, and window cornices which were unusually fine, the corner cupboard being fitted with carved shell top and ox-bow shelves. This, quite a desirable piece, sold for $70.00. Mantels brought $15.00 each, and the window cornices $12.00 a pair. I noticed on leaving the sale, that my friend who had formed the pool was dividing the purchases among his pals, and I had no regrets that I was not mixed up with them.

May 24th, 1904

THIS MORNING, while driving over to Barrington, New Hampshire, in search of antiques, I saw a lady who had a blue plate in her hand from which she was feeding her chickens. She was striking on the side of this plate and calling, "Chicky—chicky—chicky!" I said, "Be careful, Madam, you will break that plate."

She said, "I don't care if I do! For I have a cupboard full of plates like this in my pantry."

I said, "Will you please let me see what the plate is like?" And upon examination, I found it was "The Landing of the Pilgrims" and tried to purchase them. She remarked that she did not care to dispose of them, but she might consider any offer that I would care to make. I never succeeded in purchasing the plates, but I recall it as one of my early experiences in locating rare old china.

June 10th

RECEIVE A CALL from a gentleman who was anxious to purchase a Salem chest. Not knowing what the chest was like, I inquired as to its size, shape, and the manner in which it was built. He told me that they were usually made of mahogany wood, but sometimes were of native wood, as maple or birch. He described the chest as having four drawers, the corner having a carved or fluted recessed paneling, the base being finished with bandy legs and club feet.

Taking up my search for a Salem chest, I called on an acquaintance of mine who lived in the vicinity of Salem, Massachusetts. He told me that he had what he considered a genuine Salem chest of drawers. Upon looking at it, I concluded that it was the identical piece

Tuck, on the left, with his friend and whist partner, the
artist Louis Norton.

FALES COLLECTION

that my customer was anxious to purchase. So after some little trading, I managed to secure the piece for $50.00. It was in very good condition and I sold it in its natural state for $150.00.

November 15th, 1904

ABOUT THIS TIME I became interested in securing a collection of early lighting devices. I succeeded in buying several tinderboxes. These had the old flint and steel that were used to make the spark. My next find was the early rush light, these being made of forged iron in the form of nippers. The nippers were fastened to a block, and the rush or fagots were held securely by the nippers. These were used in the days before candles. The next article was the so-called whale-oil lamp. An iron pan, filled with a rag saturated with grease formed the basis of this article. This I take to be the first lighting device.

The next progress in early lighting came with the tallow candle, with many candlesticks made of iron and pewter and brass, many of the iron ones being of forged iron, handmade. These early lighting devices were used from 1750 to 1800, when the Lucifer match was just becoming popular.

During the next ten years the early lighting devices

were made into more decorative forms of glass and silver ware. About this time the so-called screw candlestand came into fashion. It seems that the early carpenters made this form of a candlestand. Many of them were in carved wood, others being painted or decorated.

In selling these early lighting devices there seemed to be no particular price established, people purchasing them at any price that would suit their purse. I find that the screw candlestand holds the preference by collectors and sells for the highest prices $100.00 is the most that I have received for any one of the several that I have sold, although I have in mind one that sold for a very much higher price. This particular screw candlestand was owned in Carthage, North Carolina, by an old lady who wrote me that she wished to find a customer for it. I went over to the old lady's home and made an examination of her old screw candlestand, finding the letters "H. F." burned into the bottom of the stand. After quizzing the old lady as to the history of the stand, I told her that I thought the best way for her to do was to write to some party who was making a collection of such early lighting devices, for by so doing she would probably get in touch with a customer. She thanked me very much for my advice.

Several months passed and I received a very nice letter from the old lady, telling me that she had sold her candlestand to people who were overjoyed to receive it back into the family. She said, "I do not feel at liberty to tell you how much I received in payment for it, but I will say that I have been very well paid. I wish to thank you for all you have done in furthering the sale of my old screw candlestand."

May 3rd, 1912

HAVE AN EXHIBITION sale at Leonard's Galleries, Detroit, Michigan, offering rare old china, glass, pictures, and prints. Much interest was shown by the people, as there were no antique shops in the city at that time. I record the sales of pictures and prints to the automobile manufacturers.

May 7th

VISIT THE FORD MOTOR COMPANY factory, purchase a 1912 touring car. The man in charge asked me if I would like to see the car assembled. I said, "How long will it take?" He replied, "It is now 10:30. I will have a guide take you through the factory; this may take you an hour or two, and on your return your car will be ready for you."

On my return from the tour of inspection I am introduced to Henry Ford. I am wondering as I chat with him if he is or ever will be interested in collecting antiques.

Leaving the Ford factory I had an attendant accompany me out to the city limits. The next day I decided to drive my new Ford car home to Maine, thinking that I would call on the various dealers and collectors, covering the territory that I went through.

My first night's stop is at Toledo, Ohio. Do not find an antique shop here, but two or three secondhand furniture shops, where I purchase several fine old flasks. This was the first lot of historical flasks that I had found. One had this inscription: "Success to the Railroad." A picture showing a horse drawing a cart and the cart filled with barrels. On the reverse side of the flask was a spread eagle and the thirteen stars around it. The other flask was known as a Pike's Peak Flask, showing a man with a pack on his back supposed to be climbing up the mountain. The legend underneath: "Pike's Peak or Bust."

Driving on to Cleveland, Ohio, I find several antique shops on Euclid Avenue. Upon investigation I find that most of the furniture in stock is made up of English antiques. However, there are many pieces of cherry-wood furniture—in fact, I find that cherry was used in Ohio and New York State more particularly than any of the early woods in the manufacture of furniture. The dealers in Ohio tell me that they have very little call for early American-made pieces.

Going over to Niagara Falls, I find the dealers there are specializing in Indian relics and some of them have a very interesting collection of stone tomahawks and arrowheads and such-like relics, but no antique furniture.

Going down through New York State, I find Rochester has two dealers that are just starting in business, having some early American pieces, the very best of which came from Portland, Maine! (I was interested to talk with them, telling them that I had opened the first antique shop in Maine and was now making a trip through New York State.) They tell me that cherry wood is the basis of most of the furniture that they find, and that secretaries, desks, and chests of drawers are the principal articles found in this locality. Prices are averaging about 25 percent less than on similar articles found in New England. Canadaigua has a very interesting shop, specializing in old forged iron articles, as andirons, door knockers, H & L hinges, and so forth. I made very few purchases—in fact, only seven pieces of furniture, on the trip covering the distance from Detroit to Boston.

June 1st

BECAME INTERESTED in issuing an historical postcard, making arrangements with the lithographers from St. Paul, who were to publish it for me. Make interesting calls on people who have nice old furniture that they will not sell, but will allow me to photograph and tell me the interesting bits of history connected with each article. Arrange my files and memoranda for the first set of postcards, that are for the New England States.

July 6th

JOHN PILLING, an Englishman, calls at my home. He wished to sell me a collection of old English clocks, he having recently returned from a three-months' visit to his kinsfolk around Staffordshire and Kent. Inquiring about the clocks, he said, "I have imported thirty-four tall hall clocks, and my brother who lives in Kent collected the lot in ten days' time." He remarked that the clocks were found in the old homes where they were placed over a hundred years ago, and that it was an English custom at that time for a bride and groom, when they were settled in their home, to receive a wedding present of two brass kettles and a tall hall clock; that the clock cost at that time about two pounds and the

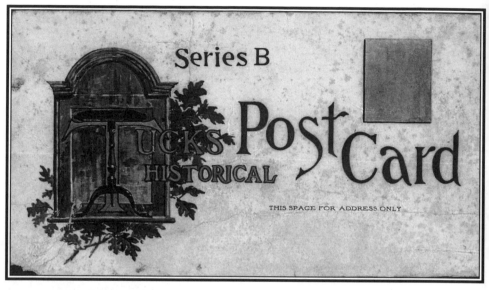

Abbott Graves painted two paintings of Tuck's shop, the one
on the cover of this book and opposite, known as *Tuck's
Antiques Shop,* and another painting titled *Colonial
Treasures,* detailing some of the items in Tuck's shop.
About 1910 Tuck began producing advertising cards and
jigsaw puzzles using the two Graves paintings and some
broadside prints of the day.

FALES COLLECTION

Tuck's Antiques Shop hangs in the Graves Memorial
Library in Kennebunkport. Alongside is a small print
marked to show the names of the local people—
besides Tuck—who posed for the painting.

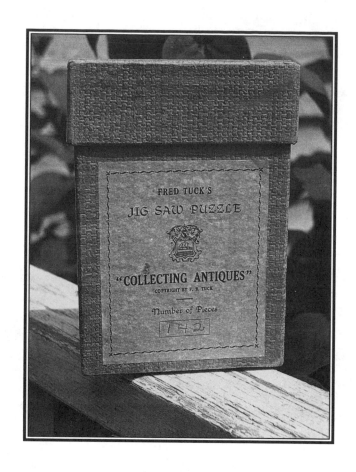

FRED TUCK'S
JIG SAW PUZZLE

"COLLECTING ANTIQUES"
COPYRIGHT BY F. B. TUCK

Number of Pieces

142

BENEDICT ARNOLD
was born at Norwich,
Connecticut, in 1741. He
is remembered chiefly by
two most unfortunate
events: his terrible march
through the Maine wilderness, on his unsuccessful
expedition against Quebec,
and his treasonable
attempt, when feeling himself wronged by Congress,
to surrender to the British
the important post of
West Point.
    He died in England in
1801, aged 61 years.

BENEDICT ARNOLD'S FURNITURE

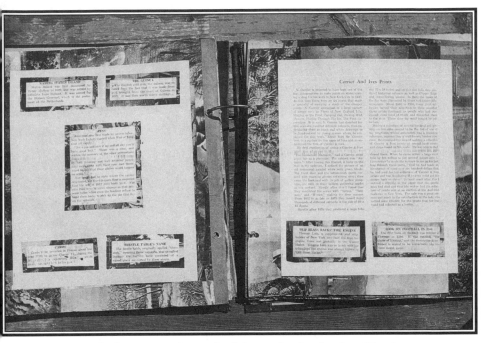

Tuck also put together colorful scrapbooks that he offered
for sale. Extremely decorative, they incorporated color
prints, newspaper and magazine clippings about antiques,
pictures of antiques and other items, various "wise" sayings, and short essays by Tuck on subjects ranging from
"The First Banjo" to "The New England Fire Bucket" to
"Old Flasks and Bottles."

FALES COLLECTION

Antiqueman's Diary

Tuck's inventiveness didn't stop with antiques. He also patented the first moth-proof garment bag.

kettle nine shillings. I became quite interested in the story of the old English clocks, and remarked that I had only American-made antiques. I was not certain that I could sell English clocks.

Mr. Pilling, taking out a notepaper from his pocket said, "I have the following items that will give you an idea as to what the clocks cost me landed in Boston. The purchase price was $8.00 each; packing ten clocks in one box, $8.00; freight and duty paid $8.00—making a total cost of $24.00 each."

Inquiring what the clocks would cost me, he said, "Well, seeing that $8.00 is the most common figure, I will accept that amount each as my profit; that is, if you will purchase the entire lot." After a few hours' consideration, I accompanied Mr. Pilling to his Massachusetts home and looked over his collection of old clocks. I was much surprised to find that many of the cases were made of solid mahogany and beautifully inlaid with colored woods, also that the brass works were apparently in good condition. I found that the clocks stood from seven to nine feet tall.

July 15th

PURCHASE THE collection of old English clocks on a basis of three clocks for $100.

December 5th, 1912

DECIDE TO OPEN a winter shop at Aiken, South Carolina. This is a very popular resort, with many of its visitors coming from New York and vicinity. Rent a store on Park Avenue. The arrangement of the store was such that the front end, fitted with large doors, could be thrown open on the level of the street. Have a very interesting stock of the various Southern styles of old furniture. Also have a collection of old silver and Sheffield plate. The old silver consisted principally of cups and mugs, and so-called hollow ware.

This particular scene opens with my sitting in the shop one morning reading the daily news, when I was quite surprised to have my attention called to a lady riding into my store on horseback. Dismounting, she said, "I am interested in these old silver cups—how many have you in your collection?"

Upon looking them over I found some eighteen or twenty that could be considered good specimens. She remarked: "I want only those with handles on them."

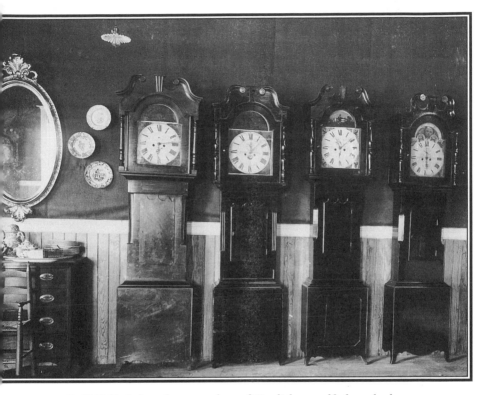

In 1912 Tuck bought a number of English grandfather clocks.
This photo, apparently taken inside Tuck's showroom, shows
clocks that are heavier than traditional American grandfather
clocks, so they could be his English bargains.

FALES COLLECTION

And, taking a strap from the horse's neck she proceeded to string as many as I found that had handles. She said, "How much will this old junk cost me collectively?"

I said, "They figure up $357.00 for the lot which you have selected."

She said, "Is that the least you will take for them?"

I said, "I will consider $325.00 for the lot." And, after she had arranged them on the pony's neck she said, "I will buy them at that price."

She then became interested in inquiring the prices of various pieces of furniture, and as I quoted her the price she remarked, "Is that the least price?"

Telling her that I had one price only on the furniture, she decides to call a little later, when she might purchase some tables. Going out by the door she spies a pair of small silver candlesticks, for the wax taper candles. This being a very small pair, I had priced them at $10.00. She thereupon asked me if that was the least I could take for them. I said, "No, Madam! In consideration of your purchases, I will present them to you with my compliments."

She, bowing very low, said, "I thank you, sir! What is your name, sir?"

I said, "My name is Tuck."

She said, "Why, that is a New England name, is it not?"

I said, "Yes, I was born in New Hampshire."

She said, "I thought I was trading with a Southerner, but I have enjoyed my interview with you, and I think I shall enjoy my purchases. I must pay you for the cups."

This she proceeded to do, paying me in gold coins. Upon taking the money I said, "To whom am I indebted for these purchases?"

She said, "My name is Mrs. Willie K. Vanderbilt, and I am very much pleased to meet you, Mr. Tuck."

A few days after having this experience with my customer who bought the cups, I was interested in receiving another visit from her. She, looking through my stock of old mahogany Southern pieces, and selecting a mahogany dressing table, a tilting swing inlaid mahogany mirror to set upon it, a pair of Hepplewhite inlaid knife boxes, and a pie-crust-top, ball-and-claw-foot mahogany table, remarked, "I think this will conclude my purchases for today." I said, "Where will you have them shipped, Madam?"

She said, "You will not have to crate them, but I shall expect you to wrap them very carefully and send them to the railroad station, where my private car will take my purchases home to New York. I think it so interesting that my old furniture, purchased in Aiken, is now going home in my private car."

During the period from 1912 to 1914 I find that the antique business is changing, in that the dealers of the North and of the South are specializing and are receiving much higher prices for the so-called marked pieces. Many are giving up the furniture end of it altogether, as they have apparently exhausted their search for the same, and are finding that the original owners are demanding too high prices for furniture for them to sell again at a profit. So they are taking up the collecting of pictures, prints, and old portraits, while others are specializing in Stiegel and Sandwich glass. About this time I became interested in collecting Currier & Ives old prints, as I had a number of calls for them the past season. I was much surprised to find the advance in price that had taken place and was at a loss to account for this, as upon investigation I found that they would not be classed as antiques, many of the highest priced ones being less that fifty years old. However, it seems there was a growing interest in collecting these pictures, and so I took an interest in finding out when and where they were made, and also how they were distributed to the general public.

N. Currier is reputed to have been one of the first lithographers to make prints in color, opening a shop in New York City about 1842. His work was principally making prints of any subjects that suited his taste, making up many subjects, and also taking photographs or views that were of historical interest. There were no art stores or places that made a specialty of selling pictures in the times of the 1840s, so a large amount of his pictures was distributed to be sold at the country stores throughout New England. Many of these pictures were retailed from $2.00 to $3.00 each; some of them were framed at that price. It has been reported to me that many of the people, when taking their country produce to the store, received a Currier & Ives picture in exchange for the balance of their produce.

About 1846 Mr. Currier took in a partner by the name of Ives, and so established the firm of Currier & Ives. From 1852 up to as late as 1875 they issued thousands of different subjects, making also a large folio. This seemed to be a specialty of the early 1870s. Numerous winter scenes, very interesting historical subjects, as well as clipper ships—in fact, the topics of the day—were

Next page: Summer bustle in Kennebunkport, circa 1914.

illustrated by these well-known lithographers.

At the present time, such-like pictures are being purchased by collectors, and seemingly large prices are paid for them. There was a collector here in Maine who, about eight years ago, decided to sell his collection, offering it at auction at the Anderson Galleries in New York. The sale was a success, and the prices were simply astonishing to people who had not made a study of the prints.

November, 1915

A YOUNG MAN called on me this morning. Said he was trying to find a pair of old leather fire buckets, but they must be a marked pair, and be dated. Turning to me, he said, "In order for me to be eligible to the fire department in our city, I have to own a pair of original leather fire buckets, and I have been having considerable trouble to find just what I want."

I told him that I did not have a marked pair. Going over to my stockroom I found two or three old ones. I made the suggestion that he purchase mine and then try and make up the pair. This he concluded to do, and so taking one of my best conditioned buckets he said, "I will see how long it will take to find one that will match this fine old one."

Two or three weeks passed, when this same young man came into my shop accompanied by his mother. He seemed quite cheerful in telling me the story of his hunt, as he had covered many miles, and finally found a bucket that would nearly match the one purchased of me. His mother remarked that she thought her son had earned his initiation to the fire department through long and patient hunting for the treasured fire buckets.

December 5, 1915
DURING THE past summer I have had many calls for writing armchairs, and not being able to supply the demand, I am turning my attention to the Southland, searching through the towns along the James River in Virginia. It seems that the first writing armchair was made in this locality by a man named Petlowe during the period from 1836 till the time of the Civil War. He planned and worked out these chairs after his own idea as to height, shape, and proportion, making some tall comb backs, and some with turned spindles for the legs. There were scarcely two alike, differing perhaps as to the shape and size of the writing lid, the cluster of braces beneath, or the spread of its legs. Some had a drawer under the writing lid, while others had a drawer between

the front legs, and still others had a drawer at the side. These chairs were often painted in plain color with now-and-then fancy decorations, or stencils.

His output for the year numbered about twenty-five, for which he averaged from forty to sixty-five dollars each. I succeeded in finding one of these Petlowe chairs of the Windsor type of build which after some little restoring I was able to sell to a man in St. Louis for $250.00. I then visited the region around Lancaster County, Pennsylvania, where I found writing armchairs with rockers made by a Dutchman. These chairs differed considerably from any that I had ever seen as they were large and heavily built and many were fitted with rockers.

The finest writing armchair that ever came to my attention was found in a minister's home at Parsonsfield, Maine. It was said to have been made for the parson and after passing through several generations of his family was bought by a dealer for $500.00. One of the features of this chair was the arrangement of five drawers in such a way as not to detract from its beauty. The chair as a whole was most unusual and so when resold brought $800.00 and finally passed into a curator's hands to be placed in a museum.

March 19, 1916

PURCHASED SEVERAL old chopping bowls at an auction. I find they have become quite popular since a lady from Camden, Maine, conceived the idea of supplying the legs taken from an old flax wheel, these legs to be fitted to the bowl thereby making it stand about two feet high. Completing this outfit, I am showing the finished chopping bowl on legs to a prospective customer. "What is that bowl used for?" she inquired.

"It can be used as a tray to hold the sewing and darning stockings, or in the library as a newspaper rack, or in the den for general catch-all."

"Oh," my prospective customer said, "I think that will prove a very useful antique. What is the price of the bowl?"

"$25.00," I said.

"I think I will purchase two," she said. "You may send one to my daughter, who lives in St. Louis, and one to my cottage at Prout's Neck."

July 10th, 1916

FRANK HOWE called this morning with a truckload of antiques. One of the articles that interested me slightly was an old cobbler's bench. Inquiring if there was any demand for this sort of an article, Howe said that he had sold five so far, but this particular one he had considered the best of the lot because it had a back that was fashioned over the seat, and this was a very unusual feature to find on a cobbler's bench. I said, "What do people use them for?"

"Well, they use them standing in the den and around the fireplace for holding pipes and cigarettes, and many use them for a tea stand, serving afternoon tea and sandwiches. Of course you understand that they are to be nicely fixed up—that is, the woodwork scraped and the seats reupholstered in leather. When they are all fitted they will sell from $10.00 to $25.00 each."

This seemed to be a freak antique to me, but as it was an unusual one, I purchased it.

I was interested the other day in calling on a dealer in New York who is making a speciality of old hat-boxes, in some districts known as bonnet boxes, and in Boston known as bandboxes. Upon looking over his collection I find that he has some twenty different subjects. Upon investigation I find that the paper is of the hand-blocked printed type, size ten by nineteen inches. After having been blocked out they were colored in by hand. On many of the sheets there were scenic views,

Forefathers Spring-House was apparently owned by F. B. Tuck in the 1920s and may have been the source for the bottled water he sold in patriotic red, white, and blue bottles.

FALES COLLECTION

taken from the different parts of New England and the middle States. One particularly interesting one was the Battery at New York; also the Deaf and Dumb Asylum at Hartford, Connecticut; another, the balloon ascension off Sandy Hook; also the dormitories at Yale College. These taken together, seemed to be an interesting antique article.

I asked him about the price that he was selling them for. He said that he would not care to set a price on this collection at present. I then decided to look around to see what I could find in old hatboxes, and I succeeded in finally finding three that were in very poor condition, the material of which they were made being of such a fragile nature that they had been badly worn in usage.

A few months after this I pick up the morning paper and note the following: "Particular interest of a particular collector."

Reading on, it said that Henry Ford had visited Boston, and in making a round of the antique shops, the articles that he purchased were principally hoop skirts and old hatboxes. Evidently he had found many to his liking, as it said that he spent some fourteen hundred dollars among the antique dealers in Boston.

Noting this, it caused me to look around for old hatboxes, in some sections known as bonnet boxes, and in Pennsylvania known as bandboxes. During my searching in the New England states I did not find any that were in good condition. But in Pennsylvania I purchased a very fine collection. I have made a study of them and I find that a feature is the interesting pictures that appear in colors on the hatbox; also that the morning paper was pasted inside the box to mark the date of issue, and that in many of the boxes that I have found the dates appear to be from 1824 to 1836. It seems that after this latter date machine-made boxes came into vogue, and so the interest in those has never been keen to collectors.

Being in New York, I spied some in a window at a Fifth Avenue millinery shop. Going in, I told the lady in attendance that I was interested in her old hatboxes. She remarked, "I will call the Madam, sir."

Presently the Madam appeared, saying, "What can I do for you, sir?"

I said, "I am interested in the old hatboxes in the window."

She curtly replied by saying, "Those are bonnet boxes, sir! They belong to one of the first families in New York, sir! They are very valuable, sir! But they are not for sale. Good-day, sir!"

Taking leave, I concluded that the man who was collecting old hatboxes must be making a speciality indeed.

The next article that came to my attention was the collecting of old liquor bottles. I was surprised one morning at my Southern store to receive a call from a gentleman who inquired of me, "Have you any old liquor bottles?"

A confirmed bachelor, Tuck had been renting a room in the
George Varney home off York Street in Kennebunk when he met
and married one of the Varneys' daughters in 1927; he was sixty
and Alice Varney was fifty-one.

FALES COLLECTION

Antiqueman's Diary
134

I said that I didn't know whether I had or not. "Possibly there are some old bottles around the shop, but I am not sure that they are what you are looking for."

He remarked that he had been interested in collecting all sorts of antiques, but he had finally settled on collecting old liquor bottles, and they proved one of the most interesting of any of the articles that he had tried to find. He said, "By the way, I am on my way to Louisville, Kentucky, where I have got on track of some fine old flasks."

Finding him a very interesting gentleman to talk with, I thought I would like to find out what kind of bottles I should buy, or what kind of flasks would be saleable to collectors. He told me that there had been a book published that I should read, and that it would tell me what style of flasks were made in the olden days. I asked him what I should pay for bottles that were illustrated in this book. He said, "Well, you will have to get your information as to value from your experiences in collecting. I would recommend that you start buying bottles of some reliable dealer, making as good a trade with them as you can. Then you could establish your selling price."

After this interview I looked around to find old bottles, but was not very successful. In a few weeks' time

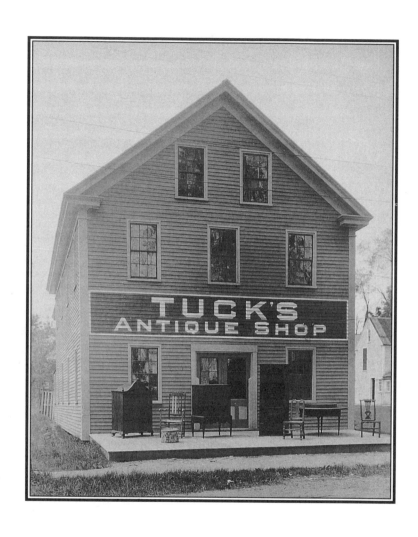

In the mid 1920s Tuck moved his shop to a York Street building
once used by his father-in-law for manufacturing plows.

several ladies came into the shop inquiring for old flasks. Then I had a man come into the shop who came from Pittsburg. He was very enthusiastic over collecting early blown bottles, so I decided to make a trip in search of old liquor bottles.

Going over to Louisville, Kentucky, I purchased several flasks at $6.00 to $10.00 each. At Wheeling, West Virginia, I ran into a large collection, purchasing the lot at $4.00 to $8.50 each. I remember some of the bottles were early blown glass with the pontil points at the bottom, the sides of the flasks portraying figures of a statesman's head. Others had flags and emblems in blue and sea-green colors. One very pretty one of calabash shape showed a bust of Jenny Lind. On the reverse side [was] a picture of the Milleflora Glass Factory where the bottle was blown. Looking it up I find the bottle was made in 1852, this being the time that P. T. Barnum brought Jenny Lind to this country as the Swedish Nightingale. Then I found Jackson and Taylor bottles, also a Louis Kossuth, picture of the frigate ship. I also found what proved to be a very desirable bottle, called the North and South, gotten out at the close of the Civil War for a gin distillery in Baltimore, Maryland. This bottle had figures of the clasped hands on the front, thirteen stars, and the word "Union." On the reverse side a dove bearing the olive branch, from a ribbon in her mouth the word "Peace." Taking my collection as a whole I found it was most interesting.

Upon opening my store at Pinehurst, North Carolina, I was quite surprised to find the interest that was shown in collecting old flasks. I secured considerable information from my many customers, who, as collectors, purchased in quantity. One gentleman who had purchased two hundred and fifty dollars' worth of me, told me that I had several rare bottles, and he was very glad to purchase and add them to his collection, saying to me, "Do you know how the collecting of old liquor bottles came about?"

I told him that I did not. He said, "By the way, it seems there was a student a few years ago at Princeton University. He had made a collection of old bottles, and was using them as a decoration in his room. Many of the bottles were given to him, others he paid a few cents for, never paying more than a dollar for what he considered his best flask.

"At the end of his college course, and when the Volstead Act was at its height, he advertised his collection for sale, and he was successful in selling his collection to a man in Delaware for $8,000. This was considered such an unusual event that a reporter came to interview him, and wrote up the history of the young man's collection. After this article was published, the bottle market became exceedingly active, and I was one of its first converts."

I thought this very interesting, and found the story helped me in the future sale of bottles.

November 1920

THIS PAGE WILL be devoted to the story of the old round dining table with a so-called "Lazy Susan" revolving top. The principal feature in describing this table is to be brought out in telling of its former history and the general history that goes with this particular table that I purchased in North Carolina and afterwards sold to a gentleman from St. Louis, who purchased the table to be used for displaying his collection of Indian relics.

Here, Tuck pauses in his memoirs, and apparently never finished them. The story of the "Lazy-Susan" table ends mid-spin.

AFTERWORD

There is an old adage in the world of antiques that New England is the attic of America, and that, in turn, Maine is the attic of New England. Certainly Fred Tuck enjoyed this advantage in his pioneering career as a dealer in "rare and curious articles" which began at the age of eighteen in 1885. By opening a shop in Kennebunkport's Union Square in 1893, he earned the distinction of being Maine's first full-time antique dealer. When Tuck died sixty years later in 1953, the state's antique business was flourishing, with shops lining Route One from Kittery to Calais.

In the Maine of the 1950s, I had the opportunity to know several memorable dealers from the generation that followed Tuck. As the result of a precocious interest in history and a passion to experience it through tangible artifacts, I made my first foray into an antique shop in the summer of 1955 when I was six years old. Returning from a family trip to Quebec City, I begged my parents to stop at a shop on the main street of Bingham, which I had spotted on our way to Canada. A friendly middle-aged couple, Barbara and Maurice Alkins, presided over neatly arranged aisles of glass, china, lamps, clocks, and furniture, along with picture-covered walls and an adjacent barn full of larger items.

The fascinating world of objects that the Alkins had created within their store would draw me back to Bingham many times in the coming years. But on that first visit, I focused my attention on a print of Gilbert Stuart's Athenaeum portrait of George Washington in a rustic Victorian frame. Naively believing that I may have discovered an original painting, I told my parents that this was the one present I wanted for my seventh birthday, regardless of the price. The days to August 17th passed quickly, and that morning I was driven to Bingham to secure my Washington portrait for all of two dollars. Time would prove it to have been clipped from a 1932 Washington Bicentennial calendar, but I prize it to this day.

At the Alkins' shop I first learned about historical photography by finding a large carton of stereo views priced at a dime apiece. When Maurice cleaned out a house, he would deposit what views he found in this box at the back of the store. Suddenly I was confronted with hundreds of engaging nineteenth-century images of Maine cities and towns, the Civil War, Western settlement, and the far corners of the globe. The

Maine cards found in that carton formed the basis for what is today a collection of 12,000 stereo views of the state. The Western stereos provided me with my first lesson in capitalism. Purchasing Jackson views of Colorado and Muybridge views of California for ten cents each, I resold them for a dollar to collectors who advertised in the *Antique Trader* newspaper. The profit margin seemed wonderful at the time, but some of those images of Colorado mining towns and Victorian San Francisco are now each worth hundreds of dollars forty years later.

As my interest in collecting grew, my parents and I explored many of the shops in Central Maine during the summer months we spent at our cottage near Skowhegan. One of the highlights of each season's rounds was the shop run by Barbara and William Kenniston in an old schoolhouse in Pittsfield on the then principal route from Skowhegan to Bangor. In the high-ceilinged main room, the Kennistons attractively displayed hundreds of choice pieces of glass and china on shelves located in front of large multi-paned windows, while the walls were hung with prints and paintings. A smaller room at the rear overflowed with clocks, furniture, and more pictures. From behind a counter in the main room, Mrs. Kenniston dispensed stereo views, post cards, photographs, and highly informative conversation which reflected a deep interest in her work. She and my mother enjoyed long talks together, and on one occasion Barbara shared a personal treasure with us, a collection of vividly written Civil War letters by one Hiram Roscoe Brackett from Detroit, Maine. Because Barbara kept these prized manuscripts in a chest of drawers near the counter, my mother always referred to the Brackett letters as "courage from an old bureau drawer."

In front of their shop, the Kennistons maintained a display of larger objects to attract passing motorists, including a rack of china chamber pots. One afternoon a young couple from New Jersey enthusiastically purchased a large flowered chamber pot for twenty-five dollars with the expressed intention of using it to serve spaghetti and meatballs, apparently innocent of the object's original purpose.

What started as a summer recreation soon became a year-round pursuit, and before long I was haunting the antique shops of my native Portland. On Saturday mornings during the school year, I would take the bus into the city and start my rounds at Sam Cinnamon's four-story brick block on the corner of Pleasant and Center Streets. A native of Russian Poland, Sam had arrived in Portland in 1904 at the age of eleven, and five years later he joined his uncle's secondhand business. In 1925 he opened his own antique and used furniture store on Fore Street, later moving to the large building at Gorham's Corner that still bears his name. Sam was a small, energetic man with an outgoing personality and a twinkle in his eye. Both he and his pleasant wife Mamie, who frequently spent the day with him at the shop, were always well dressed and attentive to customers amid a profusion of merchandise which filled four floors of what had been a cold-water Irish tenement. Sam had known members of my mother's family, including my grandfather, and he always found time to talk with me as well as to sell me whatever old photographs of Portland I found at a bargain rate of a dollar apiece. These included the earliest known photograph of Portland Head Light dating from 1858.

Sam Cinnamon handled many Portland estates during his decades in business, from which came notable furnishings and paintings. One of his most devoted customers was Judge Arthur Chapman of Cape Elizabeth, who once purchased a Fitz High Lane marine painting from Sam for fifty dollars. When Judge Chapman's estate was auctioned in the 1960s, the sale of the Lane for $10,000 electrified the Maine antiques market. Today that picture would bring at least a million dollars.

A short walk from Cinnamon's would bring me to F. O. Bailey, located in a hip-roofed brick Federal house at Free and South Streets. The Fox House was one of the last remnants of the fashionable Free Street neighborhood, and it provided an appropriate setting for the city's oldest auction firm.

Founded in 1819, Bailey's had been purchased by the Allen family in the late nineteenth century and had been run by Neal Allen, Sr., since 1912. Like Sam Cinnamon, Neal Allen knew members of my family; and when I started to frequent Bailey's, he treated me graciously. A tall, distinguished looking man in his seventies, he conducted himself in a warm and courtly manner. His well-ordered first-floor showroom displayed the best in glass, china, furniture, and paintings which Portland had to offer, its appearance being reminiscent of the better Charles Street shops in Boston. Less organized but equally intriguing were the second-floor rooms and the huge warehouse on South Street.

Neal Allen, Sr., and his staff, which included his son Franklin Allen, were indulgent of my interest in Portland history and sold me local photographs and ephemera for modest prices. At one point, Mr. Allen priced a fine lithograph of Abraham Lincoln for me at five dollars, and another time he allowed me to buy a thirty-dollar Currier and Ives print in five-dollar installments.

As a summer reporter for the *Portland Press Herald*, I covered Bailey's three-day auction of the Kenneth Roberts estate in Kennebunkport in July of 1967. By then eighty-two years old, Mr. Allen opened the sale to a round of applause. Terming the sale the most perfect of his nearly sixty-year career, he auctioned off the first eleven items of pewter before turning the gavel over to his son Franklin.

After a sandwich and a strawberry ice cream soda at W. T. Grant's lunch counter, Bentley's Restaurant, or Moustakis's Soda Fountain, I would complete my Saturday tour by walking to the Portland Street shop of Ruth Boyd. In many respects Ruth was the most colorful Portland dealer of her time. Born in St. John, New Brunswick, she came to the city at the age of five in 1902, graduating from Portland High School in

1917. Her maiden name was Gibson, and she had cut an attractive figure in her youth, resulting in the accolade of "Gibson girl" after the artist Charles Dana Gibson's popular depictions of American beauties.

During the 1920s Ruth's outgoing personality and good looks often found her included in official greeting parties for famous people visiting the city, and she cultivated these contacts when she opened Longfellow Antiques at 86 Portland Street in 1933. She made sales and sent gifts of antiques to presidents, governors, military leaders, and show business personalities. Her specialties were lamps and post cards, and her shop as well as her vintage station wagon were packed with both. Navigating Longfellow Antiques was accomplished through narrow paths shoulder high in accumulations which would have made the Collier brothers feel at home. My destination in this chaos would be the numerous shoe boxes of post cards on the shelves which lined the walls. From these boxes for a nickel apiece, I began a collection of Maine post cards which now numbers more than fifteen thousand architectural images of houses, buildings, and street scenes.

Ruth Boyd worked tenaciously at her trade well into old age, dying in 1996 at the age of ninety-nine. Her morning routine consisted of a visit to the Salvation Army, Goodwill, and any house or yard sales listed in the papers. Promptly at one o'clock, she opened her shop for four hours of afternoon business, sitting on the stoop in the warmer months and in her heated station wagon during the winter because there was no room left for her in her store. Ruth also took the direct marketing approach with her established customers. For example, if she found a good piece of pewter, she would bring it straight to the Portland collector Dr. William A. Monkhouse while he was having lunch at the Hospital Pharmacy. Transactions were concluded on the spot.

And Ruth had the last word for those who might look a bit askance at her appearance, her shop, or her car as the decades began to take their toll. One day she overheard a man in the Miss Portland Diner on Marginal Way point her out as "the old lady who runs the junk shop," and she turned to him and snapped, "Yes, and I'm the old lady who goes to the bank every day."

Fred Tuck helped pave the way for the dealers of my youth and for a business which is now an integral part of the Maine identity. The state's image as a source for significant antiques is reflected in the internationally respected *Maine Antique Digest*, which Samuel Pennington of Waldoboro has published since 1973. Each summer hundreds of shops and dozens of auctions confirm that the attic of New England still offers its treasures, just as it did in Tuck's time.

Earle G. Shettleworth, Jr.

Maine Historic Preservation Commission

ACKNOWLEDGMENTS

Our thanks to Sam Pennington; Joyce Butler; Sandy Armentrout; Marcie Molinaro and Roz Manguson at the Brick Store Museum; Ellen Moy at the Kennebunkport Historical Society; and Linda Wade at Graves Memorial Library.